Credits

Author
John P. Doran

Reviewer
Dan Weiss

Acquisition Editor
Erol Staveley

Commissioning Editor
Yogesh Dalvi

Technical Editors
Mausam Kothari

Vaibhav Pawar

Copy Editors
Insiya Morbiwala

Laxmi Subramanian

Project Coordinator
Suraj Bist

Proofreader
Elinor Perry-Smith

Indexer
Priya Subramani

Production Coordinator
Shantanu Zagade

Cover Work
Shantanu Zagade

About the Author

John P. Doran is a technical game designer who has been creating games for over 10 years. He has worked on an assortment of games in teams from just himself to over 70 in student, mod, indie, and professional projects.

He previously worked at LucasArts on *Star Wars 1313* as a game design intern. He later graduated from DigiPen Institute of Technology in Redmond, WA, with a Bachelor of Science in Game Design.

John is currently a software engineer at DigiPen's Singapore campus and is tutoring and assisting students with difficulties in computer science concepts, programming, linear algebra, game design, and advanced usage of UDK, Flash, and Unity in a development environment.

This is his third book after *UDK iOS Game Development Beginner's Guide* and *Mastering UDK Game Development*, both of which are also available from *Packt Publishing*.

He can be found online at http://johnpdoran.com and can be contacted at john@johnpdoran.com.

I want to thank my brother Chris Doran and my fiancée Hannah Mai, for being supportive and patient with me as I spent my free time and weekends away from them as I had to spend time writing the book.

On that same note, I also want to thank Samir Abou Samra and Elie Hosry for their support and encouragement while working on this book, as well as the rest of the DigiPen Singapore staff.

I want to thank Erol Staveley who approached me for writing again as well as everyone else at Packt who were so helpful, as always!

Last but not the least, I'd love to thank my family as well as my parents, Joseph and Sandra Doran, who took me seriously when I told them I wanted to make games for a living.

About the Reviewer

Dan Weiss is currently a programmer working at Psyonix Studios in San Diego, CA. He is a 2010 graduate of DigiPen Institute of Technology, having worked on titles such as *Attack of the 50ft Robot!* during his time there. He has been working in the Unreal engine since 2004, independently producing the mod *Unreal Demolition* for Unreal Tournament 2004 and Unreal Tournament 3. At Psyonix, he has been involved with Unreal engine work on mobile devices, having released ARC Squadron for iOS devices.

www.PacktPub.com

Support files, eBooks, discount offers and more

You might want to visit www.PacktPub.com for support files and downloads related to your book.

Did you know that Packt offers eBook versions of every book published, with PDF and ePub files available? You can upgrade to the eBook version at www.PacktPub.com and as a print book customer, you are entitled to a discount on the eBook copy. Get in touch with us at service@packtpub.com for more details.

At www.PacktPub.com, you can also read a collection of free technical articles, sign up for a range of free newsletters and receive exclusive discounts and offers on Packt books and eBooks.

http://PacktLib.PacktPub.com

Do you need instant solutions to your IT questions? PacktLib is Packt's online digital book library. Here, you can access, read and search across Packt's entire library of books.

Why Subscribe?

- Fully searchable across every book published by Packt
- Copy and paste, print and bookmark content
- On demand and accessible via web browser

Free Access for Packt account holders

If you have an account with Packt at www.PacktPub.com, you can use this to access PacktLib today and view nine entirely free books. Simply use your login credentials for immediate access.

Table of Contents

Preface

The UDK, which is a free version of the popular and award-winning Unreal 3 engine, is an amazing and powerful tool to use for projects of any kind. You can use it to create high-quality games and make your dream games a reality. UDK can be a little intimidating based on the level of games it has contributed to the ever growing and exciting world of gaming. Overcome all your apprehensions with this step-by-step guide and build a complete project within the Unreal Development Kit with unique gameplay, custom menus, and a triple A-rated finish.

This book will help you create a custom Tower Defense game within UDK and a game you can show your friends, even if you have absolutely no prior knowledge of UDK game development.

In next to no time, you will learn how to create any kind of environment within the UDK. With your basic environment created, you will make use of simple visual scripting to create a complete Tower Defense game with enemies attacking in waves. We then finish off the game with custom menus and a Heads Up Display. The final step is to release your game into the world and give others the excitement of playing it.

What this book covers

Chapter 1, Augmenting the UDK, introduces us to the UDK and helps us create our gameplay environment out of nothing but making use of CSG and briefly touching on Kismet to create third-person gameplay.

Chapter 2, Tower Defense, teaches us how to implant the basic gameplay for our project making use of Kismet to spawn enemies, and how to create spawnable towers in the game world making use of prefabs.

Chapter 3, Detailing Environments, discusses the role of an environment artist doing a texture pass on the environment. After that, we will place meshes to make our level pop with added details. Finally, we will add a few more things to make the experience as nice looking as possible.

Chapter 4, Finishing Touches, helps us create the basis of a Heads Up Display making use of Scaleform importing a project from Flash and touch on how to communicate between UDK and Flash. The HUD will adjust based on variables we've created in Kismet. We will also create a quick main menu level, which we can use to publish our final game! Then we will actually publish our game making use of the Unreal Frontend and share it with the world!

What you need for this book

Before we start, let's make sure that we have the latest version of the UDK (February 2013 as of this writing), which can be downloaded at http://www.unrealengine. com/udk/downloads/. When installing the program, make sure that the **UT Sample Game** option is checked.

Apart from that, all of the assets used in this project should already be included within the base UDK install.

This project and all projects assume that the user has used the UDK to some extent in the past, and is familiar with the concepts of navigating around the game environment.

For those wanting to know more about basic movement, please see Epic's UDN page that lists Hotkeys that may be useful at http://udn.epicgames.com/Three/ EditorButtons.html.

That being said, I do my best to be as descriptive as possible in the steps needed to create the game and explain why I'm doing each step.

Who this book is for

If you have ever had the urge to know more about how all those amazing games you played for countless hours are created, then this book is definitely for you! This step-by-step tutorial will teach you how to create a complete game within the UDK.

Even if you have no prior experience of the UDK, you can still start building the games you want today!

Conventions

In this book, you will find a number of styles of text that distinguish between different kinds of information. Here are some examples of these styles, and an explanation of their meaning.

Code words in text, database table names, folder names, filenames, file extensions, pathnames, dummy URLs, user input, and Twitter handles are shown as follows: "In the **Properties** window, type behindview 1 as the value for **[0]** in **Commands**"

A block of code is set as follows:

```
//Import events so that we can have something happen every frame
import flash.events.*;
//Add an event to happen every frame
stage.addEventListener(Event.ENTER_FRAME, Update);
function Update(evt:Event):void
{
  // Every frame we want to set the variables to
  // what we set them in Kismet
  cash.text = "$" + String(playerCash);
  // The wave number that we are at
  hudWaveNumber.text = String(waveNumber);
  // The times an enemy can hit our tower before we loose
  hudLives.text = String(lives);
  // If we have info to tell the player (Game Over) we can give
    // it here
  hudInfoText.text = infoText;
  // Let the player know the progress that he is making
  waveProgress.text = killedEnemies + "/" + totalEnemies;
  // The bar will fill as the player kills enemies but we don't
    // want to divide by zero so we just use a small number for
    //the scale
  if(totalEnemies> 0)
    waveBar.scaleX = killedEnemies/totalEnemies;
  else
    waveBar.scaleX = 0.01;
}
```

New terms and **important words** are shown in bold. Words that you see on the screen, in menus or dialog boxes for example, appear in the text like this: "If your viewport is zoomed in like the previous screenshot, click on the **restore viewports** button on the top right of each of the viewport".

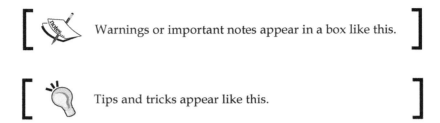

Warnings or important notes appear in a box like this.

Tips and tricks appear like this.

Reader feedback

Feedback from our readers is always welcome. Let us know what you think about this book—what you liked or may have disliked. Reader feedback is important for us to develop titles that you really get the most out of.

To send us general feedback, simply send an e-mail to feedback@packtpub.com, and mention the book title via the subject of your message.

If there is a topic that you have expertise in and you are interested in either writing or contributing to a book, see our author guide on www.packtpub.com/authors.

Customer support

Now that you are the proud owner of a Packt book, we have a number of things to help you to get the most from your purchase.

Downloading the example code

You can download the example code files for all Packt books you have purchased from your account at http://www.packtpub.com. If you purchased this book elsewhere, you can visit http://www.packtpub.com/support and register to have the files e-mailed directly to you.

Downloading the color images of this book

We also provide you a PDF file that has color images of the screenshots/diagrams used in this book. The color images will help you better understand the changes in the output. You can download this file from `http://www.packtpub.com/sites/default/files/downloads/Getting_Started_with_UDK.pdf`

Errata

Although we have taken every care to ensure the accuracy of our content, mistakes do happen. If you find a mistake in one of our books—maybe a mistake in the text or the code—we would be grateful if you would report this to us. By doing so, you can save other readers from frustration and help us improve subsequent versions of this book. If you find any errata, please report them by visiting `http://www.packtpub.com/submit-errata`, selecting your book, clicking on the **errata submission form** link, and entering the details of your errata. Once your errata are verified, your submission will be accepted and the errata will be uploaded on our website, or added to any list of existing errata, under the Errata section of that title. Any existing errata can be viewed by selecting your title from `http://www.packtpub.com/support`.

Piracy

Piracy of copyright material on the Internet is an ongoing problem across all media. At Packt, we take the protection of our copyright and licenses very seriously. If you come across any illegal copies of our works, in any form, on the Internet, please provide us with the location address or website name immediately so that we can pursue a remedy.

Please contact us at `copyright@packtpub.com` with a link to the suspected pirated material.

We appreciate your help in protecting our authors, and our ability to bring you valuable content.

Questions

You can contact us at `questions@packtpub.com` if you are having a problem with any aspect of the book, and we will do our best to address it.

1
Augmenting the UDK

The **Unreal Development Kit (UDK)**, the free version of Epic Games' Unreal Engine 3, is truly a sight to behold.

There are plenty of tutorials available on creating specific things in games, but in my experience there have been very little in terms of explaining how games are created in the actual game industry. In this book, I plan to expose those processes while creating a game from scratch using the Unreal Development Kit, including things that most tutorials leave out, such as creating menus, custom GUI, and publishing your game.

The game that we will be creating will be a basic third-person shooter / Tower Defense hybrid game using the default UDK assets. Tower Defense games have been quite popular on game sites, and we will be creating gameplay similar to that found in the popular titles Monday Night Combat and Dungeon Defenders, both of which were created using Unreal.

In this chapter, we will be creating the first playable version of our game. It will be split into five tasks. It will be a simple step-by-step process from beginning to end. Here is the outline of our tasks:

- Block out simple-level geometry
- Enable third-player mode

We will first approach the project using nothing but the UDK Editor and Kismet.

What we will achieve

Once we finish this chapter we will have the base layout of our gameplay environment done. We will also obtain a foundational knowledge in how to build areas out with CSG Brushes and exposure to Kismet before going more in depth in future chapters.

Before we begin

Before we start, let's make sure that we have the latest version of the UDK (February 2013 as of this writing), which can be downloaded at `http://www.unrealengine.com/udk/downloads/`. When installing the program, make sure that the **UT Sample Game** option is checked.

Aside from that, all of the assets used in this project should already be included within the base UDK install.

For those wanting to know more about basic movement, please see Epic's UDN page at `http://udn.epicgames.com/Three/EditorButtons.html` that lists hotkeys that may be useful.

That being said, I'll do my best to be as descriptive as possible about how to make a playable version of the game.

Block out simple-level geometry

A fitting start to our project would be to create a new level and create the area in which we want to base our game.

Prepare for lift-off

Before we start working on the project, we must first create a new map. To do this, we must first navigate to **File | New Level...**, and from the pop up that comes up, select one of the top four options (I selected **Midday Lighting**, but it doesn't matter which option you choose).

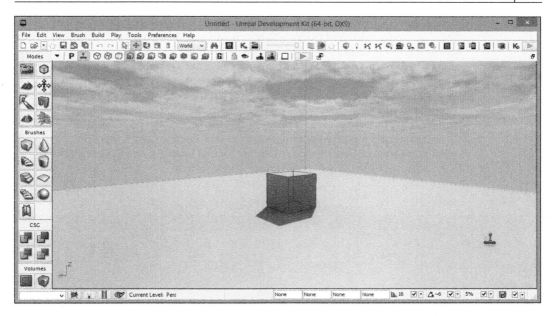

Engaging thrusters

Now that we have a base level to work with, let's start building our game! Perform the following steps:

1. If your viewport is zoomed in like the previous screenshot, click on the **restore viewports** button on the top right of each of the viewports (the icon that looks like two windows). Upon creating our level, we are greeted with a nice scene with two meshes. Let's delete this; we don't want it messing with our stuff. Make sure you click on the actual mesh and not the (red) builder brush when deleting the two objects. To delete an object, simply click on it and press the *Delete* key.

There are many different options that you can choose from to determine how the UDK is displayed and how it works for you. I encourage you to take time to figure out what you like and don't like. While having a front viewport may be nice, I like having a larger screen space for the perspective view so I have a better idea about what the area I'm creating looks like. This is more my personal preference than anything, but it is what I will be using from here on out. If you wish to follow me, navigate to **View | Viewport Configuration | 1 x 2 Split** from the top menu. For those of you using multiple monitors, you can also make use of the **Floating Viewport** option by navigating to **View | New Floating Viewport**.

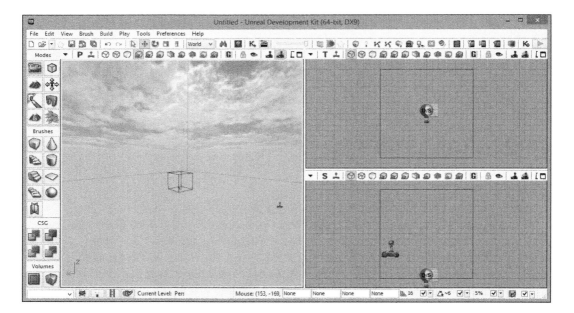

2. Once the two previous objects are destroyed, right-click on the Cube button on the top left of the **Brushes** section and bring up its dialog box. Fill in the values to create our level's floor. I used 4096 as the length (**X**) and width (**Y**) of my level with 32 for the height (**Z**).You can change it to whatever number you want, but I'd suggest you stick with a number that is a power of two (32, 64, 128, 256, 512, ...) as computers work best with them.

3. Click on the **CSG Add** button, which is on the top left of the **CSG** section in the left toolbar, in order to add the brush to our level:

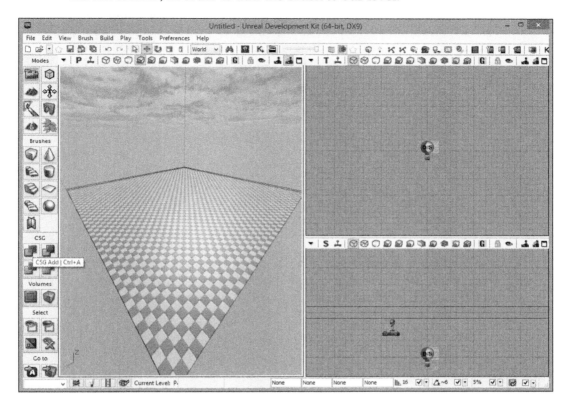

4. Next, change the **Grid Locking** amount to 32 by either using the drop-down menu or pressing *J* until you see it there from the menu on the bottom-right of the screen. Also, make sure that **Drag Grid Snap** is enabled by making sure the box next to it is checked.

Grid snapping is very useful when working on projects with the UDK. Grid snapping enables people to build brushes, making sure they are seamless with no holes in the game environment; this can make building levels much easier. You should always make sure the drag grid is enabled when working with brushes and make sure that you keep the vertices of your brushes on this grid at all times.

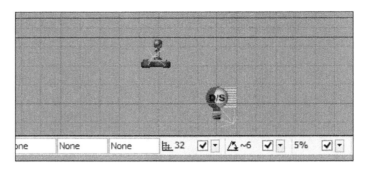

5. Press the *B* key to hide the builder brush as we will not be using it any more. Select the brush that we first created, and from the side viewport, zoom into its top-left edge and right-click on it to snap it to the grid.

 If you ever want to use the builder brush again, simply press the *B* key.

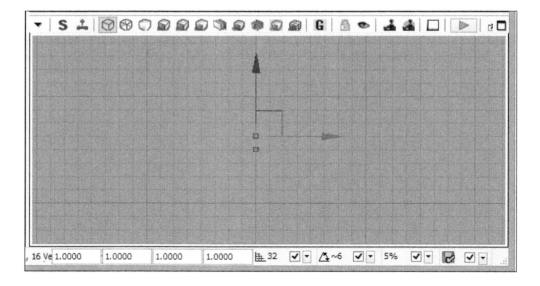

6. After that, drag it down to right below the red line you can see in the side viewport (the red line is the KillZ trigger — if a character goes below it they die automatically). Then, hold *Alt* and drag it onto the vertical axis to create a copy that is exactly on top of the previous one.

 When selecting objects using the left mouse button, holding *Ctrl* selects multiple items or deselects individual ones that are already selected; but holding *Ctrl* and *Alt* at the same time draws a marquee selection window that will be very useful in dragging terrain around.

7. Now, change the Grid Snap to 256 by pressing *]* until it gets to the correct value. Click on the **Geometry Mode** button that is located on the top right of the **Modes** section of the left toolbar. Select the two dots in the side viewport by doing a marquee selection. Once selected, drag them to the left till the block is 256 units away from the center of the level (one of the grid lines).

 A **marquee selection** is a quick way to select or deselect a group of actors within a certain area. This type of selection involves holding down a combination of keys, clicking one of the mouse buttons, and dragging the mouse cursor to create a box. All the actors within the box will be selected or deselected depending on the combination of keys and the mouse button that is clicked. The possible combinations and their effects are as follows:

Ctrl + *Alt* +left-click: Replaces the current selection with the actors contained in the box.

Ctrl + *Alt* + *Shift* +left-click: Adds the actors contained in the box to the current selection.

Ctrl + *Alt* + *Shift* +right-click: Removes any selected actors in the box from the current selection.

8. Do the same for the right-hand side. Then do the same thing for the top and bottom. By doing this, we will have created a `512 x 512 x 32` block in the center of the level. Build your geometry to see your changes by navigating to **Build | Build Geometry for Current Level**.

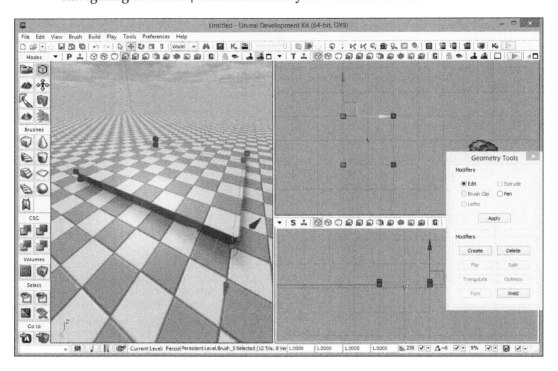

Geometry mode

This mode is immensely useful in prototyping and in making it very simple to build levels in a quick amount of time. It is always a good idea to block something out and make sure that something is fun before you spend a large amount of time creating art assets.

9. Now change the Grid Snap to 64 by pressing the [key. Now in the side viewport, left-click on only the top-left vertex (the blue box) to turn it red. Move it to the right by 64 pixels (one box).

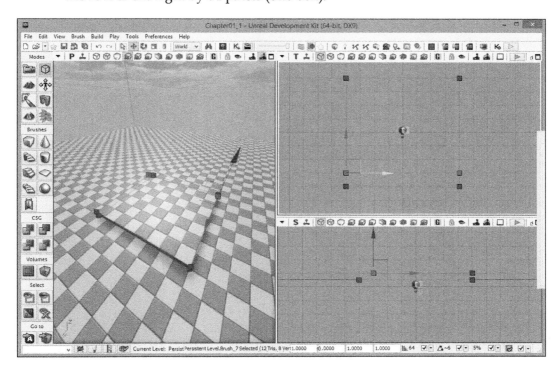

With the Geometry mode, you will not see any changes that you make in the perspective viewport until you build your project by navigating to **Build | Build Geometry for Current Level** or with the **Build All** option.

10. Now do the same with the right-hand side. After that, go to the top viewport and select the two inner vertexes on the left-hand side of the platform by a marquee selection, once again holding *Alt + Ctrl* and dragging the red box that appears over them, and move it to the left.

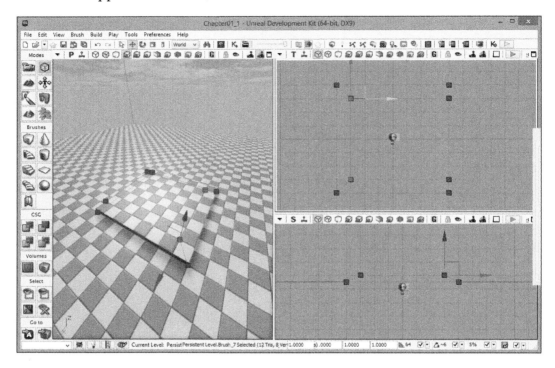

11. Now do the same on the right-hand side and then rebuild the geometry by navigating to **Build | Build Geometry for Current Level**.

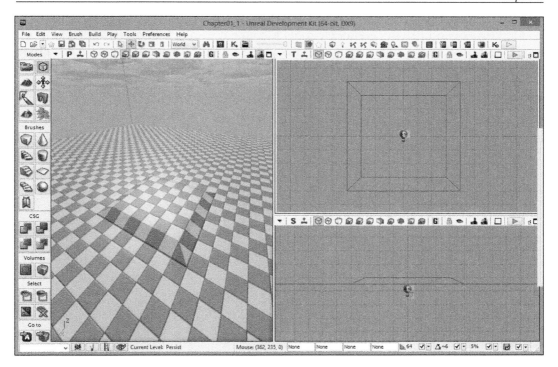

12. Bring up the **World Properties** menu by navigating to **View | World Properties** from the menu bar at the top of the UDK interface. Type Game Type in the search bar at the top of the **World Properties** menu. That will bring up the **Game Type** menu and the options relevant to us. From there, change the drop-down menus of both **Default Game Type** and **Game Type for PIE** to **UTDeathmatch**.

Now that we have the pedestal completed, let's create higher pedestals that will be the areas that the enemies cannot enter.

13. Change the grid lock back to 32 and then make another copy of the base brush, and use the geometry tools to make it 64 blocks high (two blocks at a 32-pixel snap) and drag it till it fits in the top-left corner of the level with the end around 256 pixels away from the end of the pedestal.

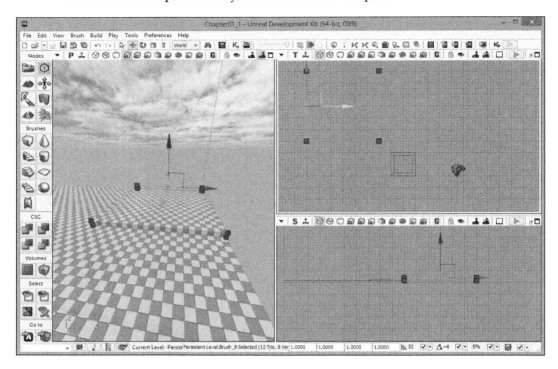

 Instead of selecting both the vertexes, it is possible to just left-click on the line at the top; you can use the transform tools in the same way.

14. After creating the pedestal, hold *Alt* and move the object to the right-hand side, creating a copy of it. Click on *Ctrl* and then click on both of them, and then clone them to the bottom half in the same way. Then build everything by navigating to **Build | Build All**.

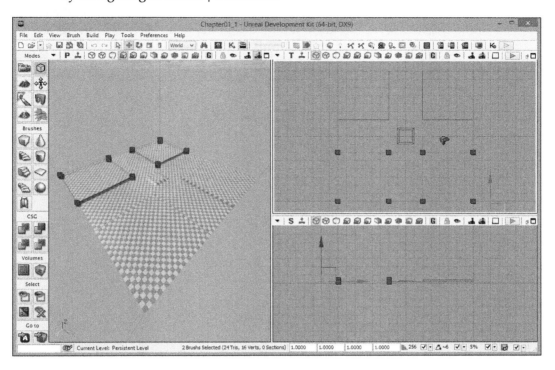

15. Now we need some way for our game to know if any enemies have gotten to our base. In order to do this, we need to add a trigger volume in the middle of our map. Press *B* so that we can see our builder brush again and then click on the **Go to Builder Brush** button that is on the right of the **Go to** section of the left toolbar. Right-click on the cylinder brush (second row on the right of the **Brushes** section of the left toolbar). In the window that pops up, set **Outer Radius** to `192` and click on **Build**.

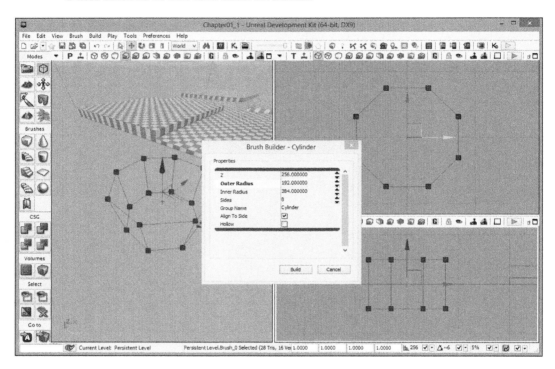

16. Move this brush to the middle of the map on the center pedestal. Now create a trigger volume by left-clicking on the **Add Volume** button (right-hand side of the **Volumes** option in the left toolbar) and then selecting **Trigger Volume**. Exit out of the Geometry mode if you are in it by left-clicking on **X** in the window that pops up. Press *B* to once again hide the builder brush.

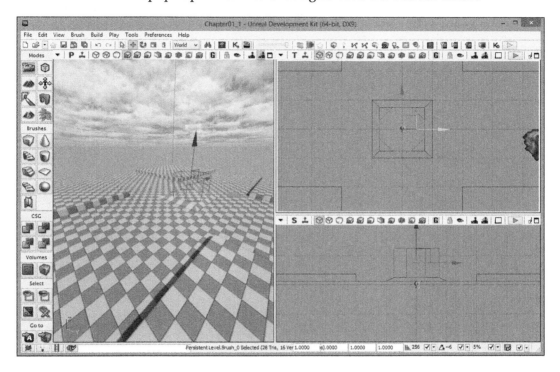

 If a brush or actor is vertically higher than the count, pressing the *End* key will snap it to the floor.

17. Finally, we're going to make pedestals to place the turrets on. Select one of the brushes that you've created already and create a copy and scale it with the geometry tools till it is 96 x 96 x 32. Place it on the left-hand side of one of the rows. Go to the side view and make a copy of it, and scale it in the **Z** axis until it is 96 pixels high. Right-click on the brush and navigate to **Convert | Convert To Volume | Blocking Volume**, and you should see it turn pink. Build the geometry to make sure that everything looks fine.

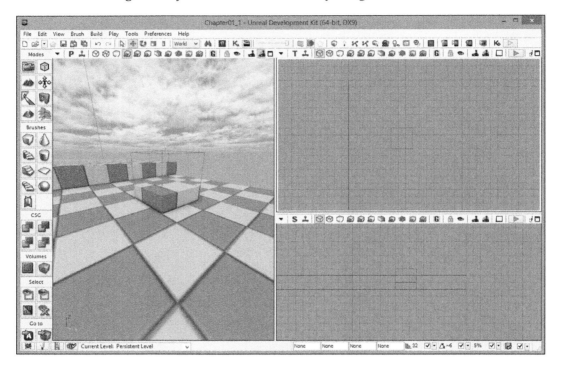

 The blocking volume is used so players and/or enemies cannot pass through the block.

18. After this, make copies of the trigger volume we made for the base and place one at the center of the pedestal; scale it up so it is about twice as big as it was before. (This will be used to tell when enemies enter the tower's range, so you can make an adjustment based on where you want them to be.)

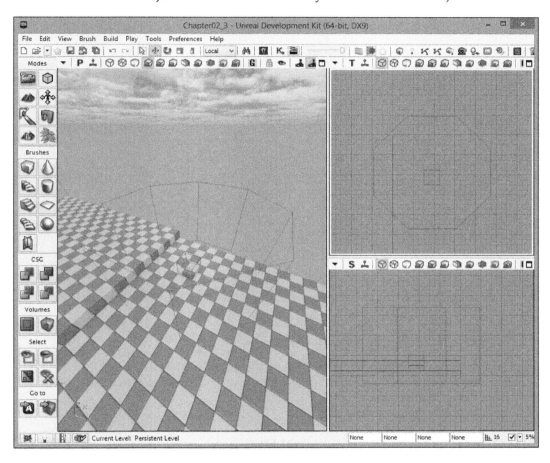

19. Build your level by navigating to **Build | Build All**. Save your project (**File | Save**) and start your game by either pressing *F8* or navigating to **Play | In Editor** on the main toolbar.

Objective complete

We have just created a very basic version of the gameplay arena that we are looking for. We've touched upon the Geometry mode and used it to create something really quickly.

Supplemental information

Now that we've used the interface to create objects in our world, let's learn how to change the default gameplay. The simplest default gameplay for the people who are just starting out is Kismet.

Defining Kismet

Kismet is a system of visual scripting in the UDK that makes it possible for people to affect the game world and design gameplay events. For teams without a programmer, Kismet can be a godsend. It makes it possible for someone without any coding knowledge to do things that would otherwise require the use of UnrealScript, the scripting language of the Unreal Engine.

In order to create a sequence of events, you will connect a series of sequence objects together. This, in turn, generates code when the game is run, which causes it to do the things that you said it should do. We will be discussing the creation of more and more complex sequences as the book progresses.

Using a third-person perspective

Now that we've learned what Kismet is and what it can do for us, let's see it used in action and see how easy it is to get results!

Engage thrusters

The default perspective given to players in the UDK is first person. Let's say we want it to be in third person instead. It will be quite easy to do so due to Epic's `console` command that does just that. Perform the following steps:

1. Open up the Kismet interface by clicking on the K-shaped icon at the top of the UDK interface on the main toolbar. You should see a new window pop up. It may look a bit daunting, but it's not too bad once you know what everything is.

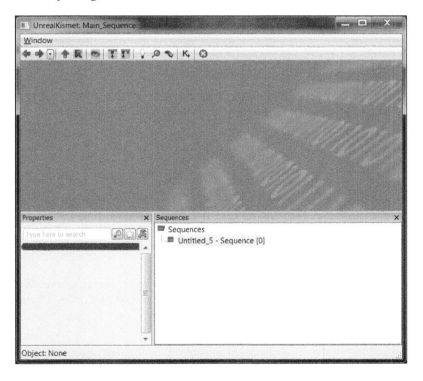

Underneath the menu bar, you will see a large area with an image of a bunch of 1's and 0's on it. This is our workspace where we will be placing all of the sequence objects we will be creating.

The bottom two bars are the **Properties** and **Sequences** windows. The **Properties** window will hold all of the data that we want to set within the sequence objects that we will be creating; they can be accessed by being left-clicked on.

2. Right-click anywhere inside the large area in the upper portion of the interface. Choose to create a **Player Spawned** event by navigating to **New Event | Player | Player Spawned** from the menu that pops up.

3. Left-click on the **Player Spawned** event to have the properties window come up and change the value of **Max Trigger Count** to 0.

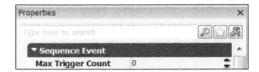

 Having a value of 0 means that it can be triggered an infinite number of times.

4. Right-click under the **Instigator** connection (the purple/pink arrow) and select **Create New Object Variable**.

5. Right-click and create a **Console Command** action by navigating to **New Action | Misc | Console Command** from the menus.

6. In the **Properties** window, type behindview 1 as the value for **[0]** in **Commands**.

 For more information on this and other console commands that you can use please see http://udn.epicgames.com/Three/ConsoleCommands.html.

7. Connect the output from the **Player Spawned** event to the input of the **Console Command** action by clicking on the black square on the right-hand side of the **Out** output on the **Player Spawned** event and dragging your mouse until it reaches the black square on the left-hand side of the **In** input.

8. Connect the connectors of both **Instigator** and **Target** to the **Object** variable we created earlier.

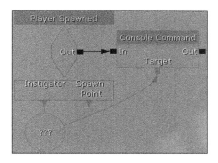

9. Save your project (**File | Save**) and start your game by pressing *F8* or navigating to**Play | In Editor** on the main toolbar.

Objective complete

Upon starting the game when the player is spawned (the Player Spawned event is activated), we change our perspective to be in the third person (the **Console Command** action is called). We've also learned some fundamentals of working with Kismet and have an understanding of how sequence objects connect together to create different effects.

Classified information

I originally wrote this section in my previous book, *UDK iOS Development Beginner's Guide, Packt Publishing*, but I feel as if it bears repeating, especially for those who have not read it before.

Kismet primer

While working with Kismet, some of the terms may be difficult to understand at first, so I would like to quickly go over some aspects of Kismet in general. Every node we work with is called a sequence object because it is an object within a sequence.

Parts of a sequence object

Have a look at the following screenshot:

The left-hand side of a sequence object is called the input while the right-hand side is called the output. Following are the variables that are either values given to us or that we set depending on the object.

There are four different kinds of sequence objects:

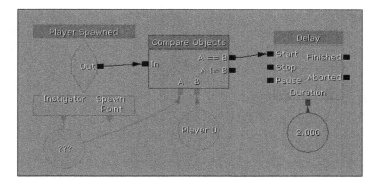

- **Events**: This is what all other sequence objects get called from. Code in Kismet, for the most part, gets called if a certain event occurs, such as the **Player Spawned** event that was called when the player spawned in our level. These objects are red and are shaped like diamonds.

- **Actions**: Actions do something when the event is triggered. This is the most used item, so it is the object with the most variety. The **Console Command** action, as well as the **Delay** variable used previously, is an example of an action. Actions are presented as rectangles.

- **Variables**: Variables hold information within our level. If another sequence object has squares underneath it, it is a spot that holds a variable. They are colored differently depending on what the variable actually is. The **Instigator** action in the Player Spawned event is a variable that is filled with our player's information when it is called, and the blue number under that **Delay** variable in the preceding screenshot is a float variable with a value of **2.0**. Variables are represented as circles.

- **Conditions**: These actions are special in the fact that they can do different things based on the values of different objects used for comparing numbers or objects. They are used to control the flow of things within a sequence. The **Compare Objects** condition is an example of a condition. Conditions are traditionally blue and rectangular.

Benefits and drawbacks of using Kismet

As with any job, it is important to use the tool that is appropriate for it. The UDK provides three applications, namely Kismet, Matinee, and UnrealScript, to make the game world more interactive. At this point, you should be familiar with the previous two options. All the three have specific advantages and disadvantages to them, but Kismet is the one that I use most often.

As you expand your research in the UDK after reading this book, you may see forum posts with people asking about how to do something in Kismet. Many people will reply to someone telling them to learn UnrealScript instead. While they may seem arrogant, there are some reasons why they are suggesting the use of this tool. I have included a list of pros and cons to Kismet that may help you afterwards in deciding if it is the correct tool for what you are working on.

Benefits of using Kismet

Kismet is a wonderful tool and is a great starting point when you are first starting with the UDK. Some other benefits associated with Kismet are as follows:

- **Has a lower barrier to entry**: No programming knowledge is needed, so it is easier to get started with Kismet and start creating games now.

- **Great for prototyping gameplay mechanics**: Saying mechanics is going to be fun is one thing, but no one is going to believe you unless you can show it. Kismet makes it extremely easy to get something up quickly. As a designer, having something to show a programmer will make it much easier for them to translate it to code.

- **Great for on-off events**: If your level needs to have something specific for an event or for only specific time or level events, such as an explosion, Kismet is a great tool to use for it.

- **Easier to see the flow of events**: If you are more of a visual thinker or like to stare at something, to see the big picture, it is a lot easier to use Kismet. The sequence objects and colors all mean something specific and make it easy to discern what is going on within a specific scene.

- **Easily extendable with UnrealScript**: With a knowledge of how UnrealScript works, it is possible to create custom sequence objects of your own to create actions of your very own. If your game would have a dialog system, creating a custom Show Dialog action would be possible in Kismet and make it easy to create entire Dialog trees within Kismet.

Drawbacks of using Kismet

However, Kismet is not the be-all and end-all solution for everything that can possibly be done with the UDK. Here are some of the drawbacks that using Kismet may have:

- **Complexity issues**: As you get more comfortable using Kismet, you will probably try to do more and more complex things with it (I know I have). If you are not careful, you may have problems reading what your code is actually doing. Basically, the more complex a sequence gets, the harder it is to read.

- **Reiterations**: Many times in a game, you will want to have the same thing happen if you are interacting with a similar or identical object, such as a door. If you want the same behavior with multiple objects (unless you use external variables) or multiple levels, you have to paste it every single time you want to that action happen. This can quickly stockpile into a really large amount of sequence objects; this can be avoided if you'll write an UnrealScript file with the same behavior and make that object use that file to execute the actions inside.

- **Level specific**: In much the same way, Kismet is also specific to just the level that it is created in. For instance, if we wanted to create 10 levels in our game, we would have had to do the **Console Command** event in every single level. With UnrealScript, this would be built into the code base for the game and be automatic for all levels of the game.

- **Kismet cannot do everything you would like to in a game**: The truth is that the game Unreal Engine 3 was created to make a **First Person Shooter** (**FPS**), and the further you stray from that path, the harder it is going to be to create your game. That has not to say that the UDK cannot be used to create other games; it's just going to be much more difficult as the sequence objects in Kismet are meant to create an FPS.

- **More custom behavior requires UnrealScript**: Continuing with the previous point, most of the time a game does something, such as a game mechanic, that the UDK does not seem to do (such as the Scarecrow boss battles Batman in Batman: Arkham Asylum, Vigorsin Bioshock Infinite, or the robot mechs in Hawken). These examples probably used UnrealScript or C++ code to achieve the desired result.

- **Kismet is slower than UnrealScript**: While it will not matter with the project that we are creating now, since Kismet is basically prewritten UnrealScript executed in a certain order, Kismet is slower than what could be achieved using just UnrealScript; and, something that your game will continuously use would best be done with UnrealScript.

Summary

A fine start to our fine project. In a short amount of time, we touched on a lot of the basic things that you will need in order to create an area quickly and effectively, which we will expand upon in *Chapter 3, Detailing Environments*. We also touched on the basics of using Kismet, which will be vital to us in the next chapter. Let's take one final look at what we have accomplished:

2
Tower Defense

Now that we have an area we can play around with, let's start taking charge of our game environment and get some basic gameplay in.

Over the course of this chapter, we will perform four tasks:

- Spawn enemies that run to the base
- Damage our base and create a Game Over scenario
- Create/Spawn a single tower
- Easily create multiple towers with prefab

With that said, let's get started!

Spawning enemies

Now that we have the basic world and a functioning player, it would be a good time to start adding things that the player can actually fight against. In this section, we will be spawning enemies and giving them a behavioral pattern.

The first step to take in order to create enemies is to first create the points in which the enemies can be created. To do this, we will create **PathNodes** to act as spawn points:

1. First, go to the menu bar at the top and access the **Actor Classes** window by going to the top menu and navigating to **View | Browser Windows | Actor Classes**. From there, select the class **PathNode** by left-clicking on it and closing the window.

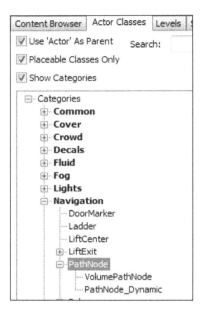

2. From here, go to the perspective viewport and right-click between one of the two raised pillars at the end. Now select **Add PathNode** here.

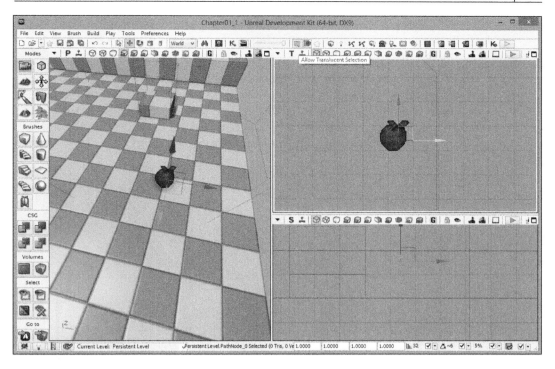

Notice the light blue arrow pointing out from the node? This is the direction in which the object spawned from the node will face.

3. Clone the node and move it to each of the four spots that you want to spawn enemies from, rotating them so that they face the center of the map. Also, place a path node on top of the middle pedestal. Once we set it up in Kismet, this node will tell the enemies where we want them to go. Build your map and make sure there are no pathing errors.

If there are any pathing issues, move the path nodes vertically up by a tad; they don't like being too close to the ground.

4. Select the four path nodes on the edge of each path by holding down *Ctrl* and left-clicking on each of them. With these selected, go into the Kismet editor.

5. The first thing to do is to create an **ObjectList** object by right-clicking and navigating to **New Variable | Object | ObjectList**. Right-click on the **ObjectList** object that you have created and select **Insert Selected Actors into ObjectList**. You will notice that the path nodes we selected earlier are now inside the **ObjectList** object. This will be useful to us down the road, as we select where we want the enemies to come out from.

 An **ObjectList** object is a unique object that lets us access its members at runtime and can be really useful any time you need to iterate through a list of objects and/or pick something randomly.

6. Create a new **Actor Factory** action by navigating to **Action | Actor | Actor Factory**.

7. First, after making sure the factory is enabled, we need to create a new variable in place of the factory. We do this by clicking on the downward-facing blue arrow. From there, we need to select **UTActorFactoryAI**. Now, change the **Pawn Class** to UTPawn and change the **Pawn Name** to Enemy. Give the enemy a **Team Index** of 1 that will put it on a different team from our player's default of 0 so it can be fired upon. Since all the enemies are on the same team, they will not attack each other. Finally, make sure you uncheck the **Check Spawn Collision** option. Right-click on the **Spawned** output and select **Create New Object Variable**. You should see it hooked up to the variable that has ??? inside it. This is great, because when an object is spawned, a reference to it will be located here.

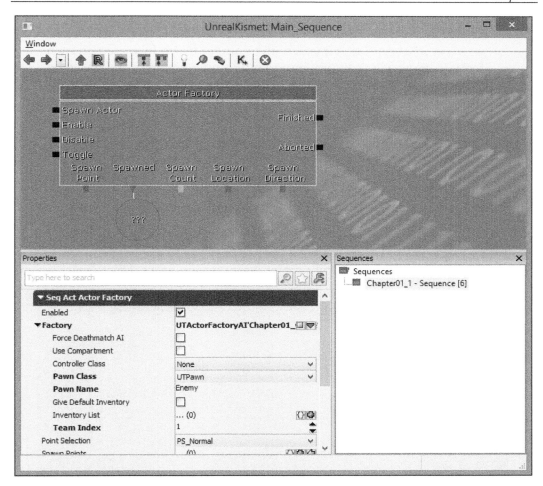

Now that we have an enemy, we need to spawn multiple enemies, tell them where to spawn, give them a place to go, and give them something to do:

1. To spawn multiple enemies, we're going to use something called **Int Counter**. Create one by right-clicking to the left-hand side of the **Actor Factory** action and navigating to **New Condition | Counter | Int Counter**.

Counters can be used to simulate a `for` loop found in programming languages, such as C. Its main function is to execute a section of Kismet, based on what condition it is in with a counter that is increased on each iteration. However, it is very importantly single-fire only, and has to be retriggered by other actions to act as a loop condition. It is very similar to the Kismet comparison **Compare Int**, but it has the added option to increment a number before the comparison.

2. Right-click underneath the outputs **A** and **B**, and create two new Int variables. Set the value of **B** to 5. (This will be the amount of enemies we will spawn before finishing the counter). Click on the **A < B** output and connect it to the **Spawn Actor** input on the **Actor Factory** action. It will not create multiple enemies until we have completed the loop, but we'll come to that later.

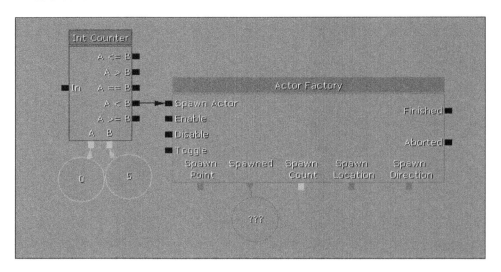

3. To tell the spawned actor to move to our base, we will create a **Move To Actor** action by navigating to **New Action | AI | Move To Actor**. Move the action to the right-hand side of the **Actor Factory** action and connect the **Finished** output from the **Actor Factory** action to the **In** input of the **Move To Actor** action. Now, connect to the **Target** connector the Object variable underneath the **Spawned** connector on the **Actor Factory** action with **???**. You can do this by dragging the purple square to the object and letting go.

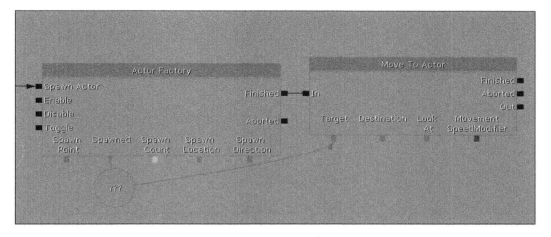

4. Exit Kismet and select the path node in the middle of the pedestal. Go back into Kismet and right-click under the **Destination** connector on the **Move To Actor** action and select **Create Object from PathNode**. Connect the **Look At** connector to it as well.

One of the neat things you can do with Kismet nodes is show values that aren't shown by default (such as the **MovementSpeedModifier** variable of the **Move To Actor** action). Since we may want to make enemies that run faster, I want to expose this variable for use in Kismet. To do this, right-click on the node and navigate to **Expose Variable | MovementSpeedModifier**.

5. If you'd like to, change **MovementSpeedModifier**; you can do so by going into **Properties** and changing it, or by exposing it and then right-clicking and selecting **Create New Float Variable** and giving the newly created float a **Value** of 0.025.

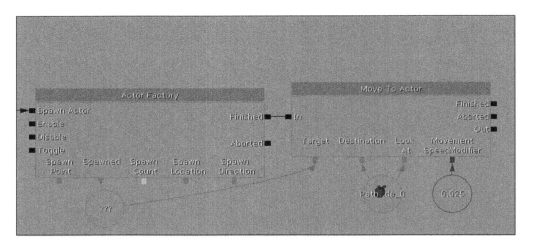

6. Now that we have the enemy created and moving to the middle of the screen, we want to spawn multiple enemies. So connect the **Out** output on the **Move To Actor** action back to the **In** input of **Int Counter**. However, we do not want enemies to spawn one after the other; we want to give some time in between callings.

 You must put a delay of some sort in between calling **Int Counter** or else the game may freeze up from calling functions so soon (0.1 seconds is usually enough).

7. One way to do this is to create a **Delay** node with a duration and connect the **Start** input of the **Delay** action to the **Out** output of the **Move To Actor** action. Then connect the **Finished** output of the **Delay** action to the **In** input of **Int Counter**, as I have shown in the following screenshot. Another way is to right-click on the **Out** output and select **Set Activate Delay**. This will enable you to set the number of seconds you have to wait before continuing with executing your actions.

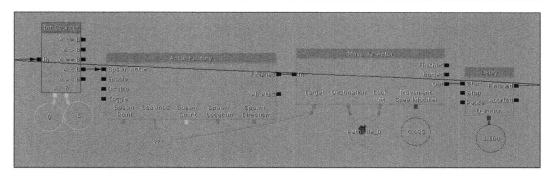

Finally, we want to set up where the enemy should actually spawn from. Now we come back to the ObjectList that we created in step 5 of the previous instruction list.

8. We need to create an **Access ObjectList** action (**New Action | ObjectList | Access ObjectList**) and place it to the left-hand side of the **Int Counter** condition.

9. Create a **Level Loaded** event (**New Event | Level Loaded**) and move it over to the left-hand side of the **Access ObjectList** action.

10. Now, connect the **Level Loaded** and **Loaded and Visible** output to the **Random** input for the **Access ObjectList** action. Connect the **Spawn Point** connector of the **Actor Factory** to the **Output Object** connector of the **Access ObjectList** action.

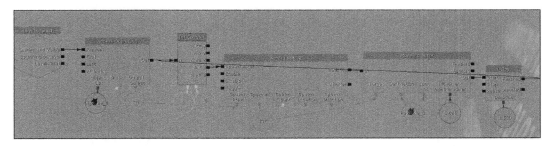

Now if we run the game, five enemies would come out of a single line and move to the center pedestal. This is all well and good, but we want to have enemies come at us continuously or in "waves". We won't go into the behavior of how waves should be created or modified in this book, but we will go over how to switch the path the enemies are coming from, and then start the counter again.

11. Now, right-click above the **Actor Factory** action and create a new **Int** action (**New Action | Set Variable | Int**). Make a new Int variable to have the value 0 and connect the **Target** connector to the **A** output on the **Int Counter** condition, resetting its value. Take the **A == B** output from the **Int Counter** condition and hook it up to the **In** input of the **Int** action.

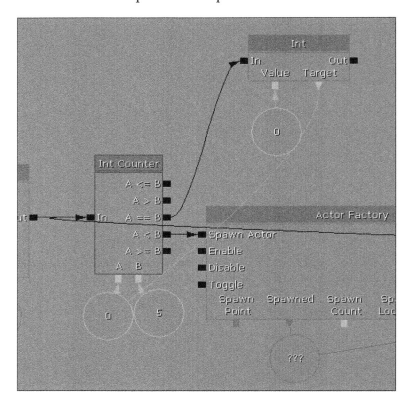

12. After this, create an **Add Int** action (**New Action | Math | Add Int**) with the **Out** output of the previous **Int** action hooked up to its **In** input. Make the **A** connector 0 (by creating a new Int variable), and under **B** create an Int variable with a value of 1. Click on the first Int variable and change its **Var Name** property to waveNumber in the action's **Properties** section. Also, connect the waveNumber variable to **IntResult** connector of **Add Int** action. Connect the **Out** output to the **Random** input on the **Access ObjectList** action.

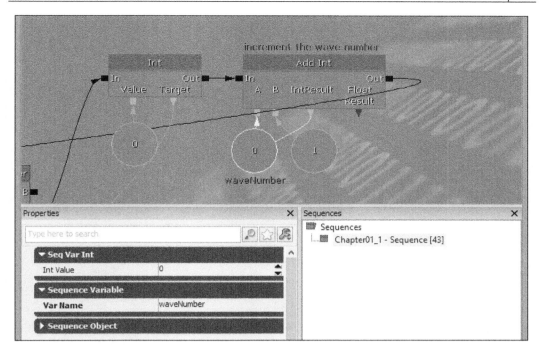

Following is a look at the entire Kismet sequence put together:

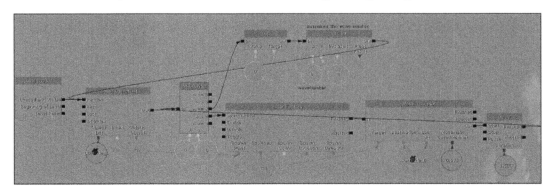

13. Build your project by navigating to **Build | Build All**. Save your game by navigating to **File | Save** and run your game by clicking on **Play** from **In Editor**.

At this point, we have a very simplistic wave system implemented, with enemies running towards the center of our map, randomly switching where they start their run from. We can attack them, and they can be defeated with a few shots.

Enemies damaging the base

Now if you were to run the game, you would see enemies that would run up to the middle of the pedestal and then perform some sort of undefined behavior. That's partially because we haven't told them to do anything yet.

We want to make the **AI** (**Artificial Intelligence**) such that upon reaching our base he destroys himself, damaging our base. His death will decrement our base's health, and upon reaching 0, we will conclude the game is over.

Now, we finally get to use those trigger volumes we created in the first section.

1. In Kismet, go back to the **Player Spawned** event we created previously, and in **Properties**, give it a **Var Name** of Player.

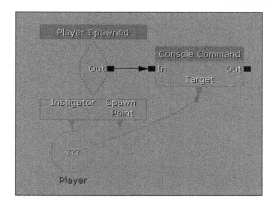

2. Exit out of Kismet and go into the editor. Select the **Trigger Volume** in the middle section that we created earlier in the first instruction list in *Chapter 1, Augmenting the UDK*. With it selected, go back into Kismet. From there, move away from your previous code and right-click on the open area and create a new **Touch** event (**New Event Using TriggerVolume | Touch**). Set the **Max Trigger Count** property to 0 (which means it can happen an infinite number of times) and uncheck the **Players Only** option. Then create an Object variable connected to the **Instigator** output.

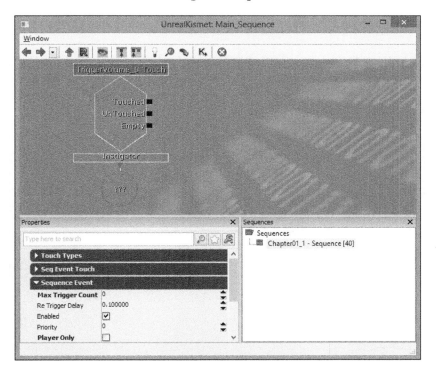

3. We want to make sure that the object that collided with the middle of the level is an enemy and not the player. We need to make a comparison to make sure it isn't. (**New Condition | Comparison | Compare Objects.**) Then, hook it up to the **Touched** output. Connect the **Instigator** output of the **TriggerVolume_0 Touch** event to **A**. Now we could draw a line to the **Player** variable I just made for **B**, but instead, we'll right-click and create a Named variable by navigating to **New Variable | Named Variable** and put in the name; this should give you a checkmark, meaning it knows what you are talking about.

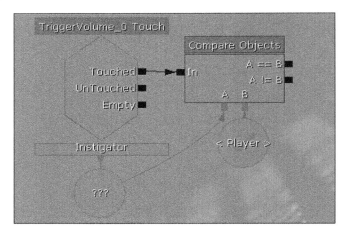

4. From the **A != B** output, attach a **Destroy** action to the right-hand side of the **Compare Objects** action by right-clicking and navigating to **New Action | Actor | Destroy**. Connect the **Target** connector of **Destroy** action to **Instigator** of the **TriggerVolume_0 Touch** event.

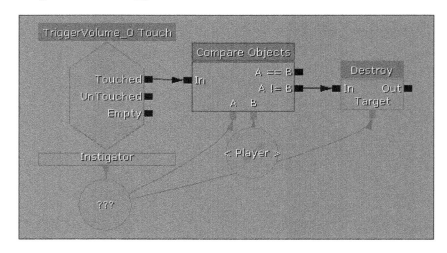

5. Create an Int variable with a **Var Name** property of `baseHealth` that will be initialized with the value of `10`.

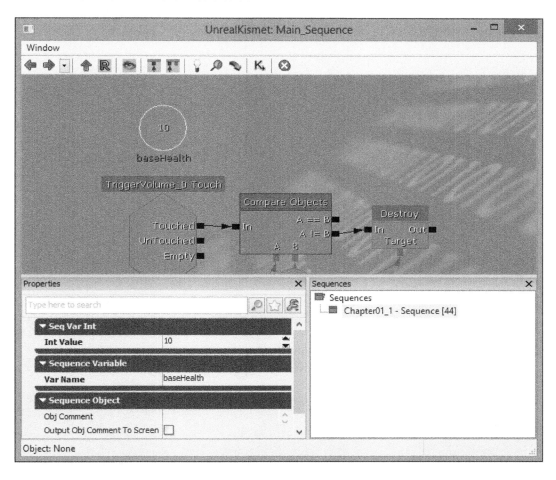

6. After the **Destroy** action, create a **Subtract Int** action (**New Action | Math | Subtract Int**) and create a named variable with `baseHealth` as the name, and hook it up to **A** and **Int Result**. In **B**, create an Int variable with a value of `1`.

7. At this point if an enemy hits this trigger, our `baseHealth` variable will be subtracted by 1. Now that players can actually lose health, let's add the functionality that if our player's health is 0 that they get some form of a `Game Over` screen.

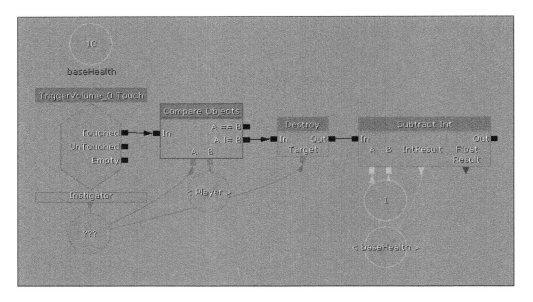

8. Afterwards, we want to compare the Int. Create a **Compare Int** condition (**New Condition | Comparison | Compare Int**) with `baseHealth` in **A** and 0 in **B**.

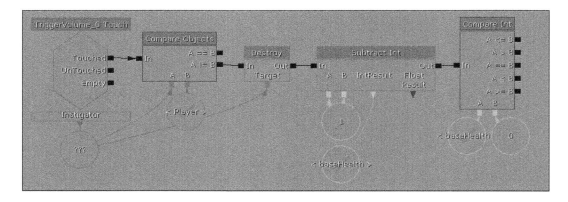

9. Create a new **Play Announcement** action (**New Action | Voice/ Announcements | Play Announcement**) and set the **Announcement Text** property to `Game Over`. Connect the **A <= B** output of the **Compare Int** condition to the **In** input of the **Play Announcement** action.

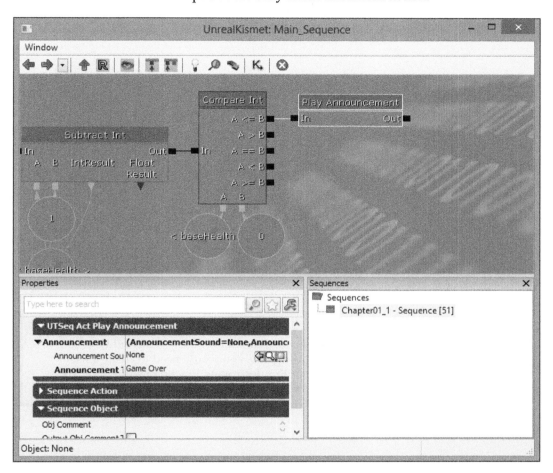

10. For debugging purposes, we may want to see when this value changes when it gets to 0. To do so, create a new **Log** action (**New Action | Misc | Log**). Right-click on the action and expose the **Int** value. Set the Int to a `baseHealth` named variable and set the **Target** to all players. (**New Variable | Player | Player**.) Then, connect the **A > B** output to the **In** input of the **Log** action.

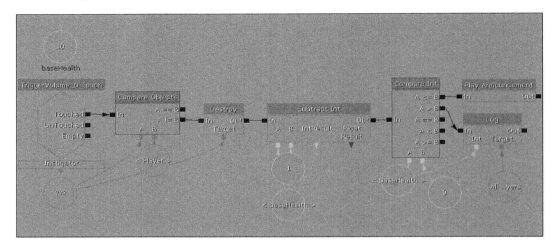

You may have noticed that we used a variable of our own called `Player` for the other parts of this function but not for this. If you would like to extend this out to a multiplayer game, you would need to create a list of players to compare against for this destroying function because the **All Players** target doesn't work when comparing objects.

11. Exit out of Kismet. Build your project by navigating to **Build | Build All**. Save your game by navigating to **File | Save** and run your game by navigating to **Play | In Editor**.

We now have a very simple Game Over system so that whenever an enemy reaches our base, they will automatically damage it. Now our game has some stakes and we won't have a bunch of enemies just piling on top of our base!

Creating/Spawning a single tower

Now that we have all of our enemies in place, we have one more mechanic to prototype. It wouldn't be much of a tower defense game without towers, so let's put them into the game now!

The first thing that we will need to do is actually create the towers. Let's do this by performing the following steps:

1. Go into the **Content Browser** window (**View | Browser Menu | Content Browser**). Check **Static Meshes** in the **Object Type** section, type in `Babel` in the search bar, and left-click on **StaticMesh'NEC_Deco.SM.Mesh.S_NEC_Supports_SM_BabelSpireA7'**.

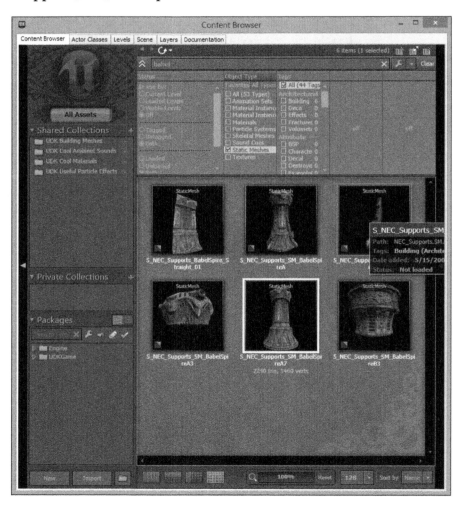

2. Exit out of the **Content Browser** window and move the perspective camera to the top of one of the pedestals we created earlier. Right-click on the pedestal and select **Add InterpActor: AEC_Deco.SM.Mesh.S_NEC_Supports_SM_BabelSpireA7**. Once created, move it to the top of the pedestal. Press *F4* to access the object's properties. Type in `Hidden` in the search bar at the top and enable the **Hidden** option in the **Display** section; in this way, the tower gets hidden from view.

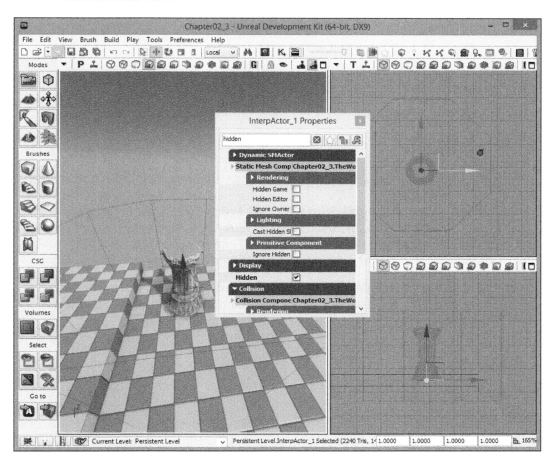

3. In order to activate our tower, we need to create a trigger. Go into the **Actor Classes** window (**View | Browser Menu | Actor Classes**) and select the **Trigger** option.

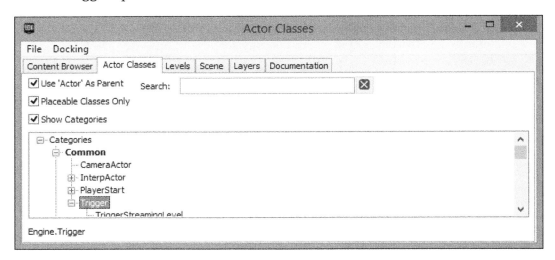

Once selected, drag-and-drop the word **Trigger** into your level and you'll see it appear in your level. Exit out of the **Actor Classes** window and then move the trigger on top of the pedestal. Then use the uniform scaling tool to increase the trigger's area to be three times larger than the original size.

4. Next, duplicate the path node on the ground by holding down *Alt* and dragging it away. Place this newly created path node on top of the newly created tower.

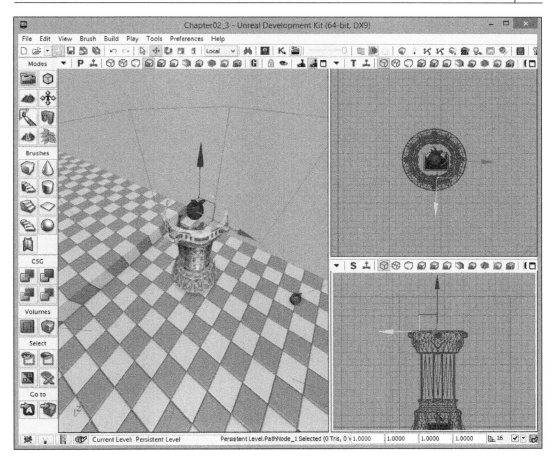

5. First, select the cylinder trigger volume that surrounds the tower. Go into Kismet and create a **Touched** action using that trigger by right-clicking and navigating to **New Event Using TriggerVolume_0 | Touch**. Inside of its **Properties** section, uncheck **Players Only** and set the **Max Trigger Count** property to 0, and create a new object variable in the **Instigator** spot.

The numbers shown in variable names are based in the order of their creation, so if you see some number instead of 0 in **TriggerVolume_0**, it's fine to use it instead.

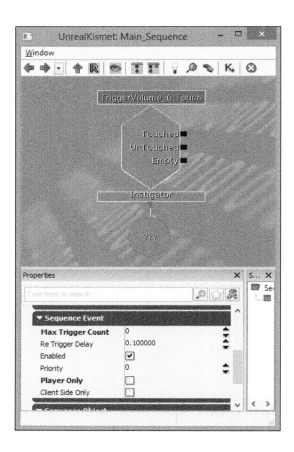

6. Next, create two **Compare Object** comparisons, one on top of the other, by navigating to **New Condition | Comparison | Compare Objects**. Connect the **Touched** output from the **TriggerVolume_0 Touch** event to the **In** input of the top **Compare Objects** condition and the **Empty** output of the **TriggerVolume_0 Touch** event to the **In** input of the bottom **Compare Objects** comparison. In the **A** section of both the **Compare Objects** comparisons, create a link to **Instigator** of the **TriggerVolume_0 Touch** event. On the top **Compare Objects** comparison for the **B** section, create a Named variable by navigating to **New Variable | Named Variable** and put in the name `Player`. For the **B** section of the second **Compare Objects** comparison, create a new object variable. Inside of its properties in the `Obj Comment` section, put **Turret Target** variable to help you understand what this is doing.

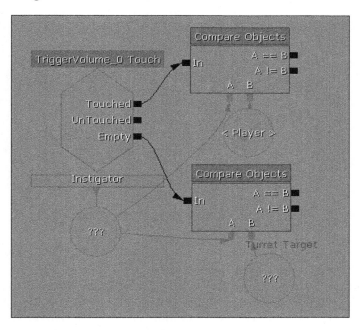

So just to explain what is going on here, whenever something touches our TriggerVolume, we first make sure that it isn't the player because we don't want to kill the player. Secondly, if an Actor leaves the TriggerVolume, the Empty state will be triggered running the Kismet that we have hooked up to it. If the object leaving the volume is our Turret's current target, we will want to find a new target for it to shoot at.

7. Create two **Set Object Variable** actions by right-clicking on and navigating to **New Action | Set Variable | Object**. Connect the **Target** connector of both actions to the variable with the **Turret Target** comment in the previous step. Connect the **A != B** output from the top **Compare Objects** comparison to the **In** input of the top **Object** action. Connect the **Value** to the **Instigator** of the **TriggerVolume_0 Touch** event. Connect **A == B** from the bottom **Compare Objects** comparison to the **In** input of the top **Object** action. Connect the **Value** connector to a new Object variable with no value.

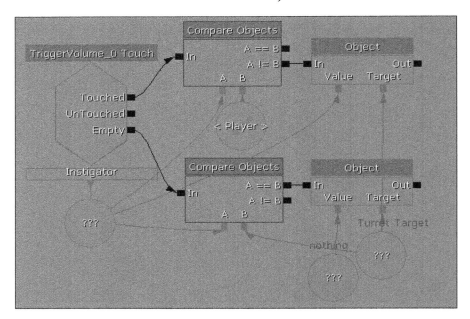

8. Create a **Destroyed** event by right-clicking and navigating to **New Event | Actor | Destroyed**. Connect the **Out** output of the event to the **In** input of the bottom **Object** action that sets the **TurretTarget** variable to nothing. Next, create an **Attach to Event** action by navigating to **New Action | Event | Attach to Event**. Under **Attach to Event**, connect the **Turret Target** variable to **Attachee** connector. Connect the **Event** connector to the **Destroyed** event that we just created. Connect the **Out** output of the top **Object** action to the **In** input of the **Attach to Event** action.

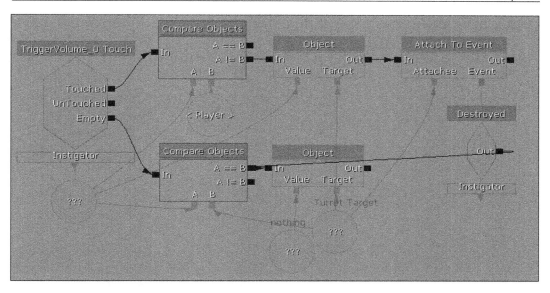

Now that we know what the object should be targeting, let's get the turret shooting.

9. Continuing with the **Trigger_1 Used** event we had earlier, we first need to create a **Toggle Hidden** event (**New Action | Toggle | Toggle Hidden**). With the **Target** being the InterpActor variable that is the tower, select it in the editor mode, right-click on it, and create its Object variable.

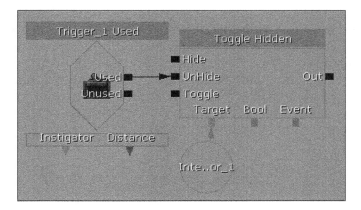

10. In the **Out** output of that place, a **Compare Objects** action comparing our **Turret Target** variable with "Nothing" (Making sure we have a target to hit). Connect the **A==B** output of this action to its **In** input with a delay of 0.2 seconds.

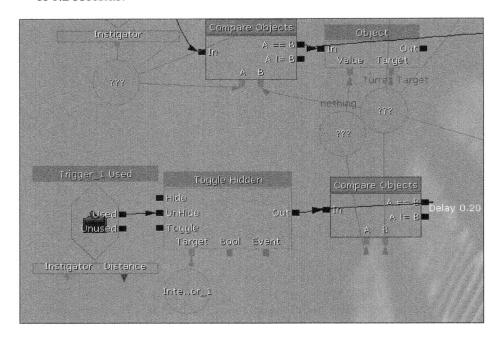

11. In the case where you do have a target, create two **Get Location and Rotation** actions (**New Action | Actor | Get Location and Rotation**). Let the first one's **Target** be the **Turret Target** variable; the other one should have the PathNode we placed above the tower (where we want the bullet to come from). Create Vector variables for both of the locations. Connect the **A != B** output of the **Compare Objects** comparison to the **In** input of the first **Get Location and Rotation** action. Then, connect the **Out** output of the first **Get Location and Rotation** action to the **In** input of the second.

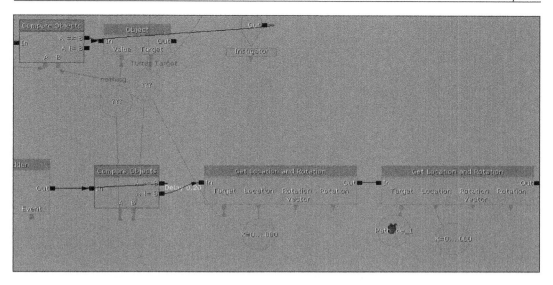

12. After getting these values, place a **Spawn Projectile** action (**New Action | Spawn Projectile**). Set the **Spawn Location** to the Path Node's location that is in the second **Get Location and Rotation** action, and set the **Target Location** to our Turret Target's location in the first. Under **Instigator**, connect the **Turret Target** variable. In the **Properties** section, set the **Projectile Class** property to UTProj_SeekingRocket. Connect the **Out** output to the **Spawn Projectile** action to the **In** input of the **Compare Objects** action to make sure you have the correct target. Add in a delay of 0.2 seconds.

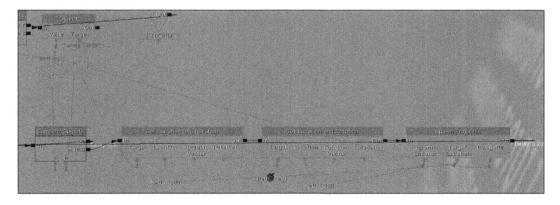

For an overview of this entire Kismet application, see the following screenshot:

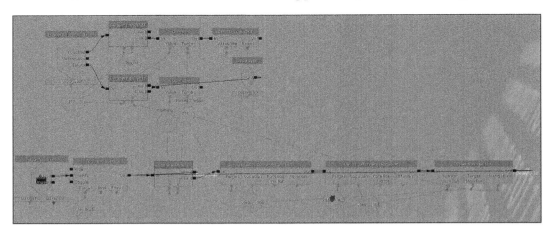

Again, remember that the level file containing all of the Kismet used is available for you to download at Packt Publishing's site in case it is difficult to view here.

13. Build your project by navigating to **Build | Build All**. Save your game by navigation to **File | Save** and run your game by navigating to **Play | In Editor**.

At this point, we now have a single podium that when activated will create a tower that will shoot projectiles at enemies that enter its radius, until they leave or the enemy is killed!

Multiple towers made easy – prefabs

Now we have created one tower, and it is a finished tower. However, we want to have many places where the player can activate towers. We can do this simply enough by making use of prefabricated objects, better known as prefabs.

Engage thrusters

The first thing that we will need to do is actually create the towers. Let's do this by performing the following steps:

1. In Kismet, do a marquee selection around all of the code we created in the previous section. Once selected, right-click and select **Create New Sequence**. In the dialog that pops up, put in the name TowerBehavior.

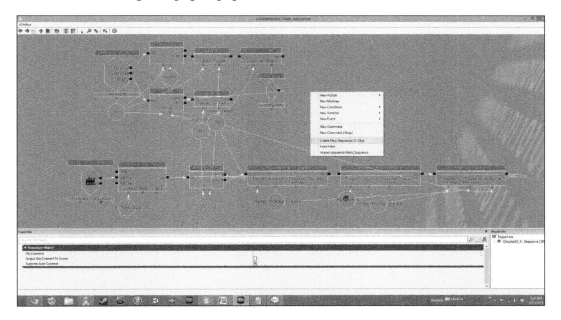

You'll notice that all of the Kismet diagrams that we created have now been put together in its own little place:

2. Exit out of Kismet and select all of the objects associated with the tower, including the `Trigger`, `Trigger Volume`, the `InterpActor`, as well as the `Blocking Volume` and **SCG (Switch Counter Groups)**. Once all of these objects are selected, right-click and select **Create Prefab** under **Package** section. Put in `TowerDefensePKG` in the **Package** field, put `TowerPrefab` in the **Name** field, and then click on **OK**.

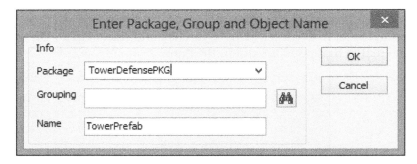

3. You will have a pop-up message saying that it found our Kismet sequence associated with this object. Click on **Yes**. Then click on **Yes** once again to replace these Actors with an instance of the prefab. As soon as this happens, go into the **Content Browser** window and save your `TowerDefensePKG` package in the same folder as your level.

4. Hold down the *Alt* key with the newly created prefab selected, and create towers along each of the lines in the pattern shown in the following screenshot:

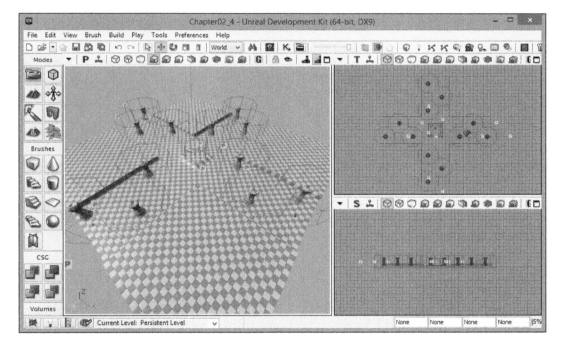

5. Build your project by navigating to **Build | Build All**. Save your game by navigating to **File | Save** and run your game by navigating to **Play | In Editor**.

At this point, we now have a single podium that, when activated, will create a tower that will shoot projectiles at enemies that enter its radius until they leave or the enemy is killed! At this point, we now have a series of podiums that can be activated for our use by doing just a few short steps!

Summary

In not too much time, we have completed some very exciting things in UDK using just the Unreal Editor and Kismet in creating a third-person tower defense title. We have the basic layout of an environment, we have enemies spawning and bombarding our base, we have a losing condition, and we have a series of points where we can activate towers. Specifically, we have spawned enemies that run to the base, damaged our base, created a Game Over scenario, created/spawned a single tower, and made multiple towers easily with prefabs.

3
Detailing Environments

One of the things that many people do not know is that level designers may actually have nothing to do with the art involved in the levels they produce. This all depends on the studio that you work at of course, but traditionally level designers are responsible for designing the gameplay that a particular level has. They develop a basic layout as well as taking care of the scripting done in the level, much like we did in the previous chapters. The actual person to create the art as well as place the art into the world is traditionally the environment artist.

At this point, our game has its core mechanics prototyped. Once prototyped, a level designer will often give his/her level to an environment artist in order to make the level more artistically pleasing.

In this chapter, we will be taking on the role of an environment artist, doing a texture pass on the environment. After that, we will place meshes to make our level pop with added details. Finally, we will add a few more items to make the experience as nice looking as possible.

This chapter will be split into four tasks depending on what we are doing. It will be a simple step-by-step process from beginning to end. The outline of our tasks is as follows:

- To apply materials to our world
- To place staircases
- To add in-level boundaries
- To spawn weapons

Applying materials

As it stands, our current level looks rather... well, bland. I'd say it's missing something in order to really make it realistic... the walls are all the same! Thankfully, we can use textures to make the walls come to life in a very simple way, bringing us one step closer to that AAA quality that we're going for!

Applying materials to our walls in **Unreal Development Kit (UDK)** is actually very simple once we know how to do it, which is what we're going to look at now:

1. First, go to the menu bar at the top and access the **Actor Classes** window by going to the top menu and navigating to **View | Browser Windows | Content Browser**. Once in the **Content Browser** window, make sure that **Packages** are sorted by folder by clicking on the left-hand side button. Once this is done, click on the **UDK Game** folder in the **Packages** window. Then type in `floor master` in the top search bar menu. Click on the **M_LT_Floors_BSP_Master** material.

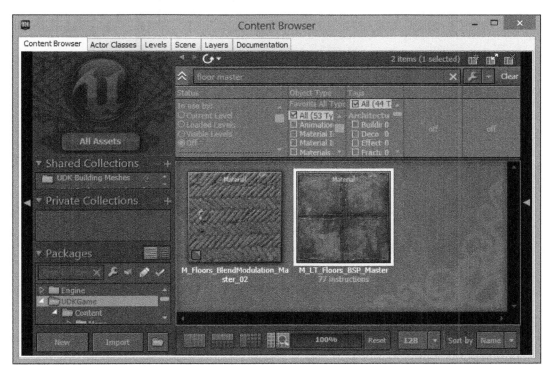

2. Close the **Content Browser** window and then left-click on the floor of our level; if you look closely, you should see. With the floor selected, right-click and select **Apply Material : M_LT_Floors_BSP_Master**.

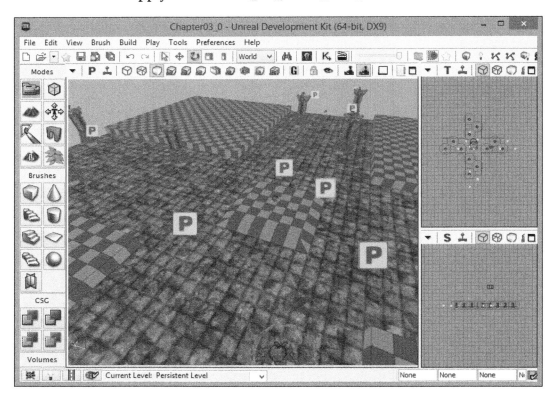

3. Now that we have given the floor a material, let's give it a platform as well. Select each of the faces by holding down *Ctrl* and left-clicking on them individually. Once selected, right-click and select **Apply Material : M_LT_Floors_BSP_Master**.

Another way to select all of the faces would be to right-click on the floor and navigate to **Select Surfaces | Adjacent Floors**.

Now our floor is placed; but if you play the game, you may notice the texture being repeated over and over again and the texture on the platform being stretched strangely. One of the ways we can rectify this problem is by scaling the texture to fit our needs.

4. With all of the floor and the pieces of the platform selected, navigate to **View | Surface Properties**. From there, change the **Simple** field under **Scaling** to **2.0** and click on the **Apply** button to its right that will double the size of our textures. After that, go to **Alignment** and select **Box**; click on the **Apply** button placed below it to align our textures as if the faces that we selected were like a box. This works very well for objects consisting of box-like objects (our brushes, for instance).

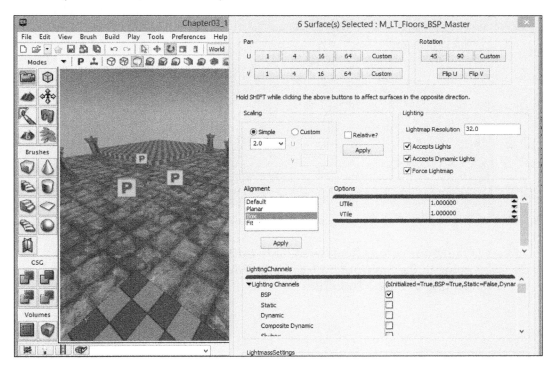

5. Close the **Surface Properties** window and open up the **Content Browser** window. Now search for floors organic. Select **M_LT_Floors_BSP_ Organic15b** and close the **Content Browser** window.

6. Now select one of the floors on the edges with the default texture on them. Then right-click and go to **Select Surfaces | Matching Texture**. After that, right-click and select **Apply Material : M_LT_Floors_BSP_Organic15b**.

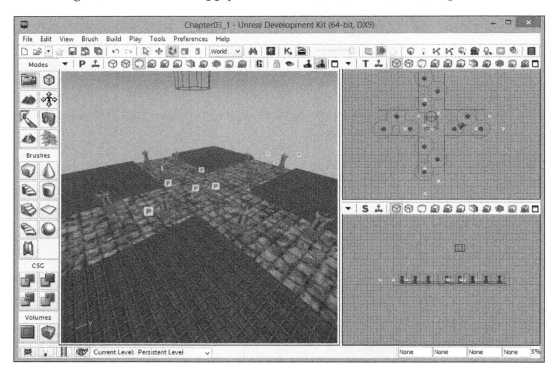

7. We build our project by navigating to **Build | Build All**, save our game by going to the **Save** option within the **File** menu, and run our game by navigating to **Play | In Editor**.

And with that, we now have a nicely textured world, and it is quite a good start towards getting our levels looking as refined as possible.

Placing staircases

Okay, our floors are very neat, but we are still missing a lot of details. For one, the player can see the level going on forever and it's a very plain level. To solve this problem, we can use static meshes. Non-moving static meshes, as their name implies, are a tool that we can use to fill a level with details at a very low performance cost.

To start with, let's create some stairs. Perform the following steps:

1. First, go to the menu bar at the top and access the **Actor Classes** window by going to the top menu and navigating to **View | Browser Windows | Content Browser**. This time, in the **Object Type** panel check the **Static Meshes** option. Make sure that you have set up the UDK Game folder in the **Packages** window. Then type in stair in the top search bar menu. Click on the **S_ASC_Floor_SM_StairsSid01** static mesh.

2. Move out of the **Content Browser** window. Move your perspective viewport over to one of the four corners in the level. Right-click on the ground and select **Add Static Mesh : ASC_Floors:S_ASC_Floor_SM_StairsSid01**.

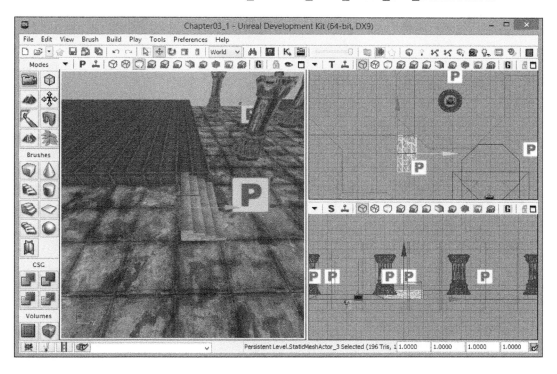

3. Change your transformation widget till you get to the rotation slide that looks like a large circle. There, left-click on the blue part of the widget and drag it until the number changes to 90 and the widget rotates our object for us.

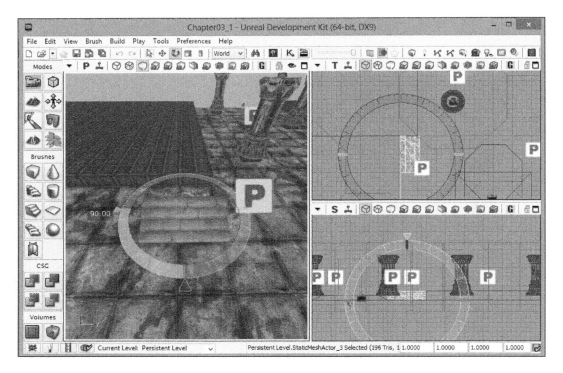

4. Now press the Space bar twice to get back to the **Transform** widget. Move the staircase until it is flesh with the edge of the wall. After that, hold down *Alt* and drag the wall down to create a copy of the stairs. Do this again and again till you cover the entire wall.

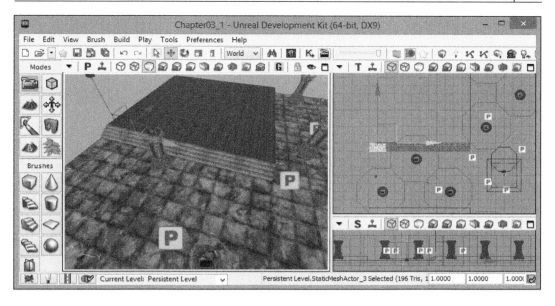

5. Now duplicate the entire row of objects and move them to the wall on the other side. To flip them, right-click and navigate to **Transform | Mirror X Axis**.

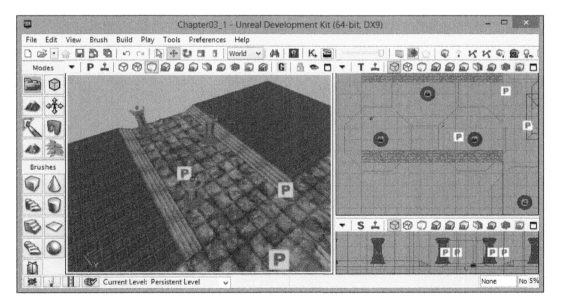

6. Select these objects, and then create another copy on the other side of the wall by holding down *Alt* and dragging the **Transform** widget in the direction you want to travel in. Select all the objects, create a copy, then rotate them 90 degrees to fill up our entire level.

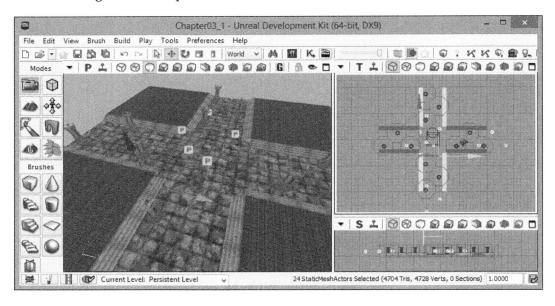

7. We build our project by navigating to **Build | Build All**, save our game by navigating to **File | Save**, and run our game by navigating to **Play | In Editor**.

8. And now we have an easy way to travel up and down our two height levels in the game, giving the player an additional choice to travel in the game.

Adding in-level boundaries

Okay, now we have a very simple example of how we can use meshes. With this fundamental knowledge, we will use static meshes to create our level boundaries.

Let's get started by finding a suitable mesh. Perform the following steps:

1. Go to the **Content Browser** window (that is, navigate to **View | Browser Menu | Content Browser**). Check the **Static Meshes** checkbox in the **Object Type** section and type in `trim vented` and left-click on **StaticMesh 'NEC_Trims.SM.Mesh.S_NEC_Trims_SM_Vented03a'**.

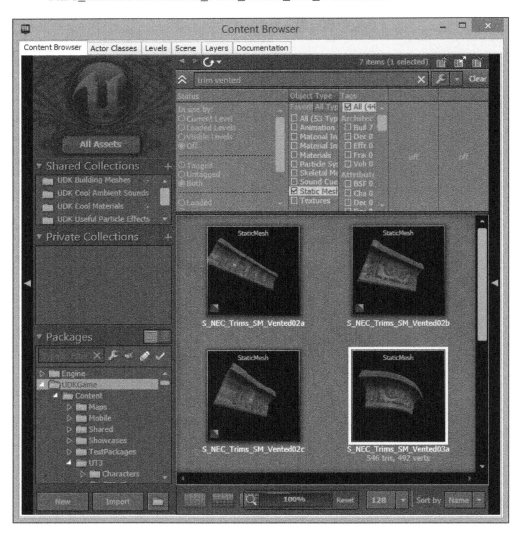

2. Close the **Content Browser** window and move the perspective camera to the end of one of our lanes. Right-click on the pedestal and select **Add StaticMesh: NEC_Trims.SM.Mesh.S_NEC_Trims_SM_Vented03a.**

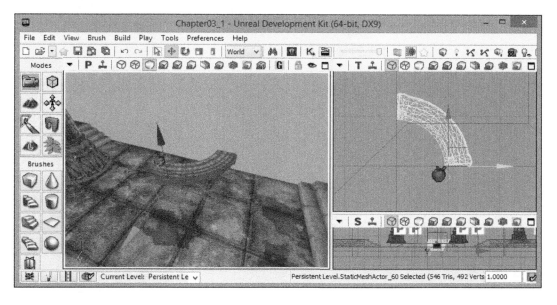

3. Once created, you'll notice that the mesh is quite small. Rotate the object 135 degrees. Open up the mesh's properties by pressing the *F4* key. Once open, change the value to **11** in the **X**, **Y**, and **Z** fields under the **Draw Scale 3D** field, using the search bar at the top to help you find it. Then translate the object so that it covers the lane it is stationed at.

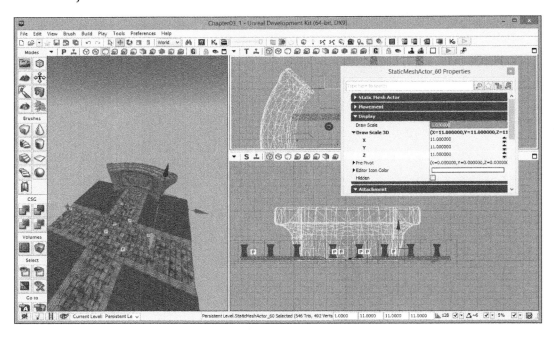

4. Now translate the object down by 256 pixels in the **Z** field. Then in the same way as we did in the previous section, create three copies at the end of each of the lanes.

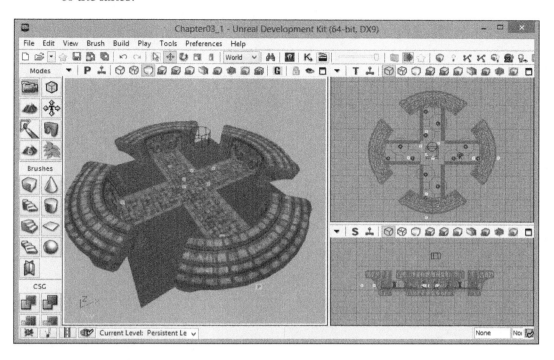

5. Now, we'll add in some ingenuity. Make an additional copy of one of the meshes, this time changing the **Draw Scale** value to **8.5** in the **X**, **Y**, and **Z** fields. Now rotate the mesh to face the opposite way. After that, make the top of this mesh flesh with the top of the other edges.

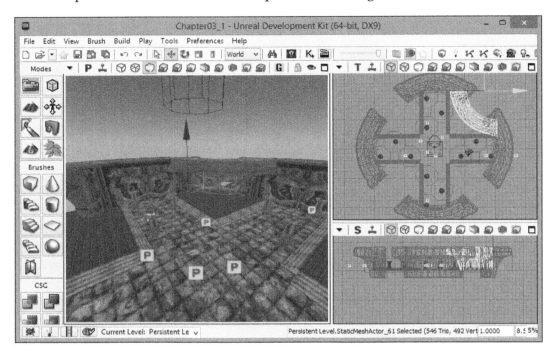

6. Now let's create three additional copies to complete our level!

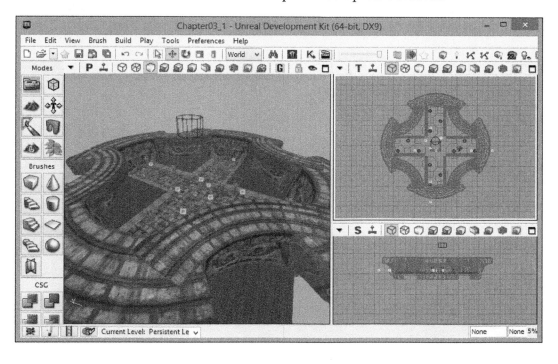

7. We build our project by navigating to **Build | Build All**, save our game by clicking on **Save** within the **File** menu, and run our game by navigating to **Play | In Editor**.

8. And now we have a very polished level to look at, with minimal work in the same color scheme, just like the rest of the assets in the game!

Spawning weapons

Now that we have a pretty level, I have one more feature to add before we continue. As the game currently is, the ammo available to a player is severely limited, increasing the difficulty exponentially. Granted, this may have been an option if we were trying to create a game where we wanted supplies to be scarce, but that's not the case.

One of the tools that level designers have is the ability to reward players for traversing certain ways and promoting certain behavior. Inside the **Actor Classes** tab, there is a class called UTPickupFactory with both health and weapon pickups. In this section, we will place weapon pickups in our level.

The first thing that we will need to do is actually create a class named WeaponFactories that will create weapons for the player to pick up. Let's do that now!

1. First, go to the menu bar at the top and access the **Actor Classes** window by going to the top menu and navigating to **View | Browser Windows | Actor Classes**. From there, type utweapon into the search bar and select the class **UTWeaponPickupFactory** by left-clicking on it and closing the window.

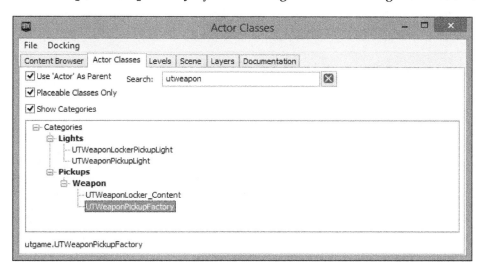

2. From here, go to the perspective viewport and right-click anywhere between one of the two raised pillars at the end. Then, select **Add UTWeaponPickupFactory** here. You may not see anything. If that's the case, drag the object on the **Z** (vertical) axis till it is above the ground and press the *End* key to have it automatically fall to the ground. Open up **Properties** by pressing *F4* and change **Weapon Pickup Class** to **UTWeap_LinkGun**.

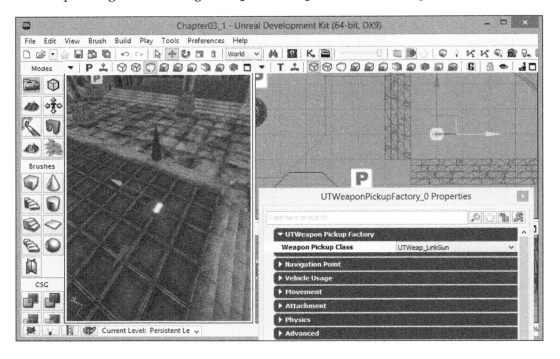

3. Create three additional copies and place them at the other edges of the upper level.

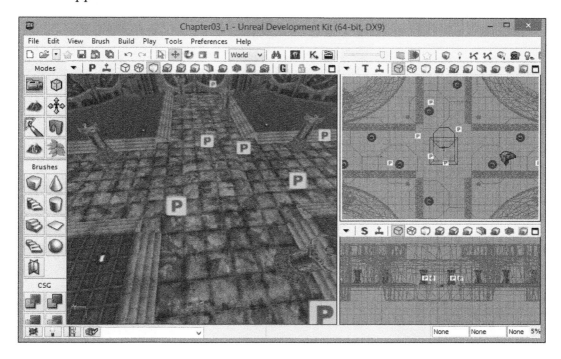

4. We build our project by navigating to **Build | Build All**, save our game by clicking on **Save** within the **File** menu, and run our game by navigating to **Play | In Editor**.

Objective complete

Now we have a level that contains pickups that will spawn! The player will have no difficulty fighting enemies now.

Summary

What a difference a little work makes! We just used some basic textures and some simple static mesh placements to quickly make a level that's quite polished! More specifically, we applied materials to our world, placed staircases, added in-level boundaries, and spawned weapons.

Next, we will take the final steps to complete our game and get it out into the world!

4
Finishing Touches

There are a lot of tutorial books out there that teach you how to perform a specific task, or how to create the basis for a project, but in this chapter we'll be covering some concepts that most books don't, that is, how to finish a game project and get it out to the world.

In this chapter, we will be finishing up our game by adding menus and publishing the game making use of Unreal Frontend.

To do that, we will be creating a **Heads Up Display (HUD)** that can provide additional information to players about our specific game type as well as a main menu for our game, making use of Scaleform and Actionscript 3.0 using Adobe Flash CS6.

At the end of this chapter, we would have created the basis of a Heads Up Display making use of Scaleform and would have touched on how to communicate between UDK and Flash using Kismet. We will also create a quick main menu level, which we can use to publish our final game! Then we will actually publish our game making use of the Unreal Frontend and share it with the world!

Over the course of this chapter we will do the following:

- Setting up Flash
- Creating our main menu
- Creating our HUD
- Importing Flash files into UDK
- Cooking/packaging the game

Obtaining Flash

Scaleform does not require us to use Adobe Flash, but this is the environment that we will be using to create our UI content. I will be using the latest Adobe Flash CS6, but we should be able to do most of the things in this chapter using a previous version. For those without Flash, Adobe offers a free trial of all of their software. For more information on that, please visit www.adobe.com/go/tryflash/.

We will also need the art assets for our menu. These can be downloaded from the **Support** page on the Packt website at www.packtpub.com/support.

Setting up Flash

Our first step will be setting up Flash in order to create our HUD. To do this, we must first install the Scaleform launcher. I have written a nice tutorial on how to install Scaleform launcher on my website, which you are welcome to look through at http://johnpdoran.com/setting-up-flash-cs6-to-use-scaleform-with-udk/.

Creating our main menu

Now that Flash is set up, let's actually create a very simple screen, our main menu.

But before we get into that, let's talk a little bit about the environment, as I'm guessing many of you may never have worked with Flash before. On my website, I have a quick overview of the features that Flash has as well as how they are normally used. To read that, visit http://johnpdoran.com/flash-101-an-introduction/.

Now that we have a basis of what Flash is like, let's get started! Perform the following steps:

1. Inside the Adobe Flash main menu, create a new ActionScript 3.0 project by navigating to **Create New | Actionscript 3.0**.

2. In the Properties inspector of the Stage properties of the **Properties** section set the size to 1280 and 720 by clicking on the existing numbers and typing in the new values and then pressing *Enter*. Above the Stage, find the **Zoom** scaling, which currently says **100%** and change it so that you can see everything within the white box. Alternatively, you can use *Ctrl + 1*.

3. Import our image files by navigating to **File** | **Import** | **Import to Library...**. From there, go to the `Chapter's assets` folder where you will find the `MainMenu_Art` folder. In that folder, select all of the files and then click on **Open**.

4. Access **Library** by left-clicking on the tab next to **Properties** in **Properties Inspector**. At the bottom-left of the **Library** tab, click on the far left button to create a **New Symbol**. Alternatively press *Ctrl + F8*.

5. In the Window that pops up, type in `gameButton` in the **Name** field of the new symbol and change **Type** to **Button** from the drop-down menu. Once that's completed, click on the **OK** button.

6. At this point, you should see **Timeline** at the bottom of our changed screen and notice that we are now inside our newly created **Button**. Keep in mind that the **+** symbol on the screen is our pivot point to the Stage when we place the button in our map. Right-click on the box below the **Over** frame of **Timeline** and select **Create New Keyframe**. Repeat the same step for the **Down** frame.

7. Select the **Up** frame again. Then go back to **Library** and drag-and-drop the `button_normal.png` image so that **+** is in the top-left of the button. You should notice that the empty circle is now filled.

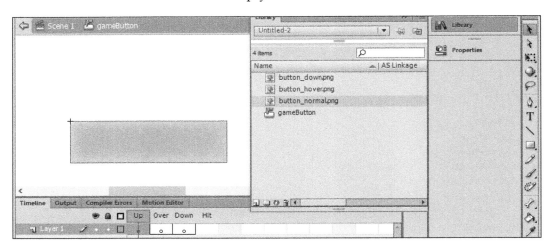

8. Next, place the `button_hover.png` image in the **Over** frame, and then place `button_down.png` in the **Down** frame. You can click on the **Properties** tab to change the position of objects where you can set the **X** and **Y** values to `0`.

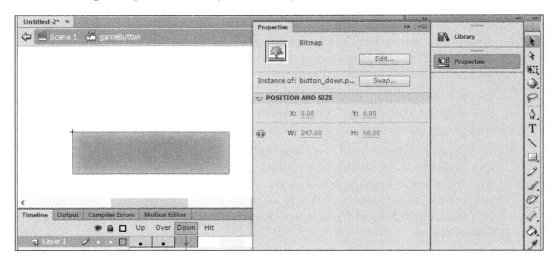

9. We are now done with our button's basic construction! Now, click on the blue arrow pointing to the left to return to our Scene. Then save your project as `TowerDefenseMM.fla`.

10. Go to **Library** and drag-and-drop our game object button onto the Stage. Then open up the **Align** menu by pressing *Ctrl + K*. Check the **Align to Stage** option and then click on the second button, which will align the object to the center of our stage.

11. Then click on the **Properties** tab with the **Button** selected. At the very top you should see some text that says **<Instance Name>**. Change that value to playButton.

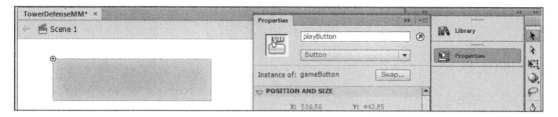

12. Now let's add the text! Click on the T symbol to use the **Text** tool. Left-click and drag to create an area of text and type in the name of your game (I used Tower Defender). Make the font size large enough so that the text is easily seen. Then under **FILTERS**, click on the bottom-left option to create a new **Glow** filter. There I changed **Color** to black to make the text easily visible in light as well as dark areas.

13. Now, click on **Embed...** next to the **Style** section of the **CHARACTER** part of the **Text** properties. In the Font Embedding screen, under **OPTIONS** check **Uppercase**, **Lowercase**, **Numerals**, and **Punctuation**. Then go to the **ActionScript** tab, check the **Export for ActionScript** and **Export in frame 1** options. When the warning comes up saying it'll generate the file for you, just click on **OK**.

14. Now copy (*Ctrl + C*) and paste (*Ctrl + V*) the text that we just created and drag it over to our button. Adjust the size of the textbox to fit the smaller area and decrease the font to a smaller size (42). Change the text to `Play Game` and then change its type from **Static Text** to **Dynamic Text**. Once this is done, you should see an instance name pop up. Change it to `playText`.

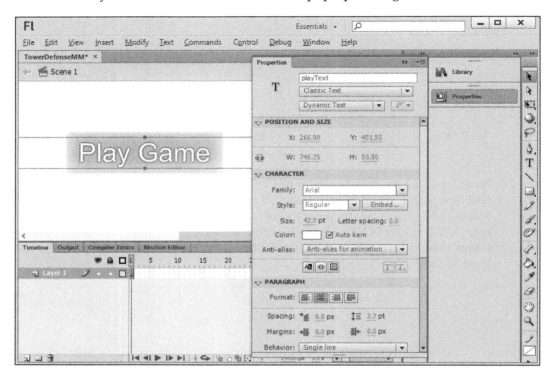

15. Now right-click on the first frame of our **Timeline** (the black circle) and select **Actions**. You should see a window popup. Insert the following code in the window that pops up:

```
playText.mouseEnabled = false;
```

This will disable mouse clicks on the text, so that the button can work.

16. Now, we need to create a mouse pointer. Instead of providing a picture, I thought it'd be a good idea to show you the drawing tools that Flash has. From the bar on the right, click on the paint bucket icon and then select a blue color.

17. Press *o* to start using the **Oval** tool. Press *Shift* and *Alt*, then click and drag out a circle somewhere inside your menu.

18. From here, go back to the **Selection** tool and left-click on the blue circle. Then right-click and select **Convert to Symbol**. From there give it a name mouse and a type named **Movie Clip**.

19. Once converted, give the newly created **Movie Clip** an instance name of mouseMC.

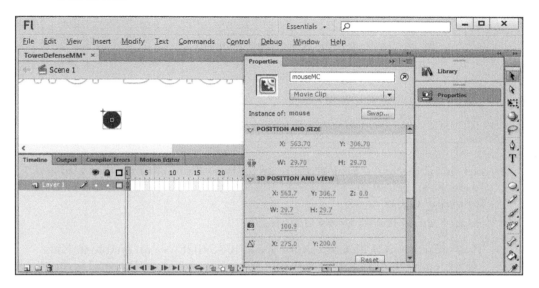

20. Also, right-click on the **mouseMC** movie clip and navigate to **Arrange | Bring to Front** to be sure that it is at the top of your movie.

21. Now, make sure you have no object selected and then click on the **Properties** tab. In **Properties**, you will see a variable called **Class**. Fill this in with the same name that we will be saving our file as, in this case TowerDefenseMM. A warning will pop up saying that a class will be generated for us. Click on **OK**.

22. Now click on the pencil icon next to the class we just named and a popup will come up asking us in which program to open the file. Make sure that **Flash Professional** is selected and then click on **OK**. You should see something similar to the following screenshot:

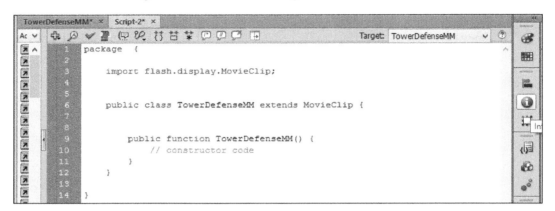

23. For this sample of a project, there are only two small things that we need to do. First, below the `import flash.display.MovieClip;` line add the following line of code:

```
import scaleform.gfx.Extensions;
```

This will import Scaleform's functionality so that we can enable it. Next, create a new line underneath the `//constructor code` line and write the following code:

```
Extensions.enabled = true;
```

This will actually enable us to use the Scaleform properly. Every Scaleform project that you'll be creating requires these two things.

24. Now go back to **Actions** for the first frame of your object on **Timeline** and add the following code to your previously created line:

```
//Import the events that we wish to use
import flash.events.MouseEvent;
import flash.system.fscommand;

playButton.addEventListener(MouseEvent.MOUSE_DOWN,
  playGame);
function playGame(event:MouseEvent):void
{
  //Tell Unreal to play the game
  fscommand('playGame');
}
```

```
stage.addEventListener(MouseEvent.MOUSE_MOVE,
  mousePosition);
function mousePosition(event:MouseEvent)
{
  // When we move the mouse, change our circle's position
  mouseMC.x = mouseX;
  mouseMC.y = mouseY;
}

stop();
```

25. Close the **Actions** tab. Then save your file and run it with the Scaleform launcher by navigating to **Window | Other Windows | Scaleform Launcher** and then selecting **Test with: GFxMediaPlayerD3d9**.

Now we have a very simple main menu screen that will respond to a mouse click on a button, which will send FSCommand to Unreal, that we can make use of later on down the road. Now, before we jump into UDK again, let's make one more thing inside Flash, a fully functional HUD system!

Creating our HUD

Now that we have the main menu created, let's create our actual game's HUD! We get started in much the same way as the previous section. Perform the following steps:

1. Inside the Adobe Flash main menu, create a new ActionScript 3.0 project by navigating to **Create New | Actionscript 3.0**.

2. In **Properties Inspector** of the Stage properties of the **Properties** section, set the size to 1280 x 720 by clicking on the existing numbers and typing in the new values then pressing *Enter*. Above the stage, find the **Zoom** scaling, which currently says **100%**, and change it so that you can see everything within the white box. Alternatively, you can use *Ctrl + 1*.

3. Import our image files by navigating to **File | Import | Import to Library...**. From there, go to the Chapter's assets folder where you will find the MainMenu_Art folder. In that folder, select all the files and then click on **Open**.

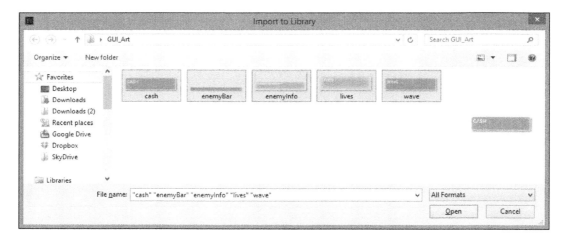

4. Access **Library** by left-clicking on the tab next to **Properties** in **Properties Inspector**. From **Library**, drag-and-drop the imported images onto the Stage of the level. Click on the wave.png (the box with the word **WAVE** in it) image and click on the **Properties** tab to bring up the options that we can use in order to alter its position. Change the **X** and **Y** values to 14 to put it at the top-left of the image.

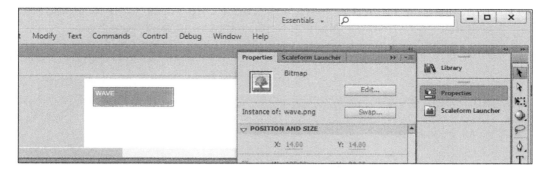

5. With the `lives.png` image, change the position to `14, 684`. Then change the `cash.png` image's position to `1114, 690`. For `enemyInfo.png`, give a position of `826, 4`. Finally, place `enemyBar.png` at `834, 12` to cover up the grey bar that `enemyInfo` has. When you are finished, you should have something that looks very similar to the following screenshot:

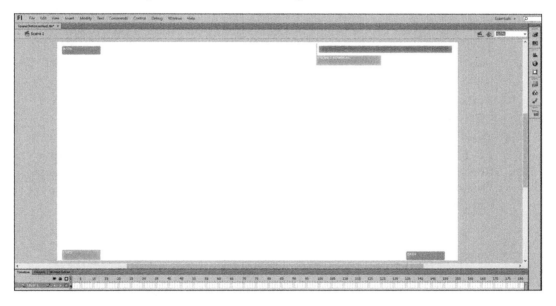

6. Right-click on the `enemyBar` image and select **Convert to Symbol**. Make sure that the converted type is a **Movie Clip** and write `waveBar` in the name property.

7. Now open the **Properties** of the new **Movie Clip**. At the top you should see text that says **<Instance Name>**. Replace that value with waveBar.

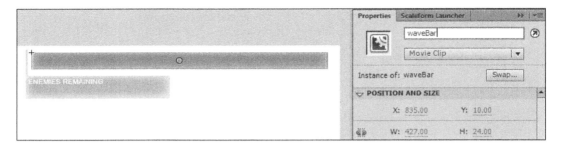

8. Click on the **Text** tool and left-click in the center of the **waveBar** that we created and drag it to the right to give it some additional space between the text we want to place. Once created, type in 10/10 just to give you some visual idea of what we are creating.

9. In the same text object's **Properties**, you will notice a new kind of window that pops up for text objects. Change the text from **Static Text** to **Dynamic Text** form by selecting from the drop-down menu. You will then notice a new **Instance Name** window popup. Inside the window, give this object the name waveProgress.

10. In the same text object's **Paragraph** section, change the text to be centered by selecting the second option from the **Align** section.

11. Then go to the very bottom of the same text object's **Properties** and go to **FILTERS**. In that menu, click on the first button on the left to create a new filter. From there select **Drop Shadow**. In the **Drop Shadow** filter, make the **Distance** field 0 and leave the other values as default; this will make our numbers easily visible.

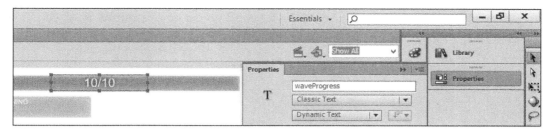

12. Now, click on **Embed...** next to the **Style** section of the **CHARACTER** part of the **Text** properties. In the Font Embedding screen, under **OPTIONS** check **Uppercase**, **Lowercase**, **Numerals**, and **Punctuation**. Then go to the **ActionScript** tab, check the **Export for ActionScript** and **Export in frame 1** options. When the warning comes up saying it'll generate the file for you, just click on **OK**.

13. Now, copy and paste the text file and drag it over to the **Wave** section at the top-left of the screen. Adjust the size of the textbox to fit in the smaller area and increase the font to a larger size (25). Change the text to 1 and the instance name to hudWaveNumber.

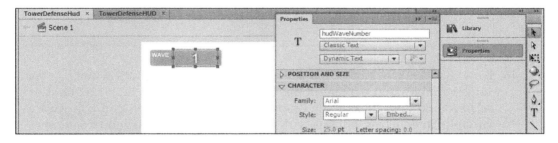

14. Make a copy of this text by pressing *Alt* and dragging them to the other parts. Fill the **LIVES** section with **10** and give it an instance name of hudLives. Create another copy of the text for the **CASH** section. Alter the size of this section so that the text area can fit **$1000** comfortably, then give it an instance name of cash.

15. Lastly, create one final copy of the text and give a large amount of space between the **LIVES** and **CASH** areas. In the textbox, type `You Win!` and give it an instance name of `hudInfoText`. Here we can give the player information, such as whether they won or lost the game.

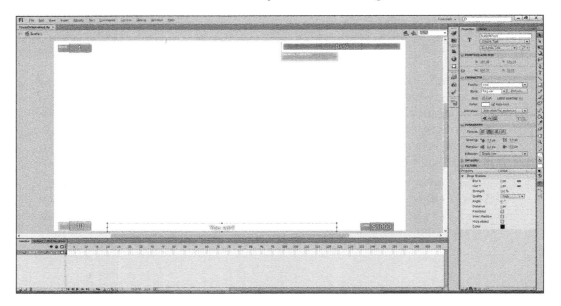

16. Now that we have all the things that will display values, let's actually create some variables that we can set this text to. Make sure you have no object selected and then click on the **Properties** tab. In **Properties**, you will see a variable called **Class**. Fill this with the same name that we will be saving our file as, in this case `TowerDefenseHUD`. This is the Document Class, which is the home class that our Scaleform will be using, and will contain the variables that we will be changing later in Kismet.

17. Click on the pencil icon next to **Class**. There may be a warning; if so, just click on **OK** and click on the pencil icon again. When it asks you what to open the ActionScript class with, select the editor and then click on **OK**.

18. From there, you will see some default code that opens inside our editor. Replace that code with the following code:

```
package
{
  //import libraries we need to use
  import flash.display.MovieClip;
  import flash.events.KeyboardEvent;
  import scaleform.gfx.Extensions;
```

```
public class TowerDefenseHUD extends MovieClip
{
  //Variables we are going to be using in Kismet
  public static varplayerCash:int = 100;
  public static varkilledEnemies:int = 0;
  public static vartotalEnemies:int = 0;
  public static varwaveNumber:int = 0;
  public static varlives:int = 55;
  public static varinfoText:String = "";

  //Constructor - Called when the flash file is played
  public function TowerDefenseHUD()
  {
    //Enable functionality of Scaleform
    Extensions.enabled = true;
  }
}
}
```

19. Once finished, save this file as well as the HUD file as `TowerDefenseHUD` in the same folder.

20. Now that we have our files saved, let's add in the functionality to adjust the values at runtime. Go to **Timeline** at the bottom of our Flash toolbar and select the first frame of Layer 1 (where there is a black circle inside the **Timeline** tab), then right-click and select **Actions**.

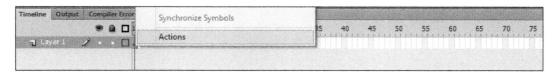

21. On selecting **Actions**, another code window will come up. Fill that window with the following code:

```
//Import events so that we can have something happen every frame
import flash.events.*;
//Add an event to happen every frame
stage.addEventListener(Event.ENTER_FRAME, Update);
function Update(evt:Event):void
{
  // Every frame we want to set the variables to
  // what we set them in Kismet
  cash.text = "$" + String(playerCash);
  // The wave number that we are at
```

```
hudWaveNumber.text = String(waveNumber);
// The times an enemy can hit our tower before we loose
hudLives.text = String(lives);
// If we have info to tell the player (Game Over) we can give
  // it here
hudInfoText.text = infoText;
// Let the player know the progress that he is making
waveProgress.text = killedEnemies + "/" + totalEnemies;
// The bar will fill as the player kills enemies but we don't
  // want to divide by zero so we just use a small number for
  //the scale
if(totalEnemies> 0)
  waveBar.scaleX = killedEnemies/totalEnemies;
else
  waveBar.scaleX = 0.01;
}
```

22. Then save your file and run it with the Scaleform launcher by navigating to **Window | Other Windows | Scaleform Launcher** and then selecting **Test with: GFxMediaPlayerD3d9**.

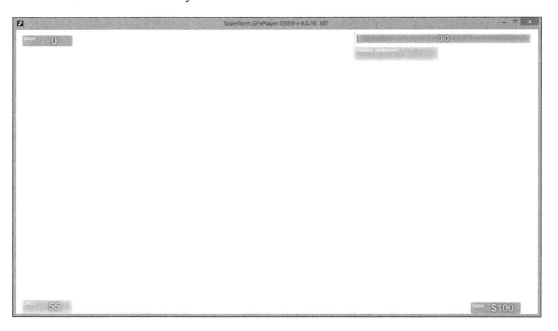

At this point we have a working and functional HUD system after we do some simple code implementation within Kismet. At this point, we are also done with Flash and can start the implementation within our actual UDK game!

Creating the main menu into UDK

Now that we have our content, let's bring it in! Perform the following steps:

1. UDK can only import Flash files that are within a specific folder. Inside your file browser, go to the folder that contains `.fla` and `.as` files that we created earlier. In that folder you should see a file with a `.swf` extension. Copy that file and go to your UDK folder at `UDKGame\Flash\` and create a new folder called `TDGame`. Inside that folder, paste the `.swf` Flash movie files.

2. Start up UDK again. Open up the content browser and click on the **Import** button. Find the movie files and click on **OK**. You'll notice that the **Import** dialog already sets the package name to **TDGame**, so just click on **OK** and save this package.

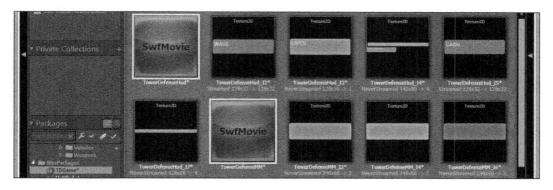

3. Now, the first thing we are going to do is to create the main menu level. First create a new level by navigating to **File** | **New Level**. From the menu that pops up, select **Blank Map**.

4. Now we still need to spawn a hero, so first right-click on the image of the box on the left toolbar under **Brushes**. Once you get to the menu, check the **Hallow** option and then click on **Build**. Now click on **Add from the CSG Menu** to create an area where our player can spawn. Finally, move the camera inside our newly-created box and then right-click on the ground and navigate to **Add Actor | Add PlayerStart**.

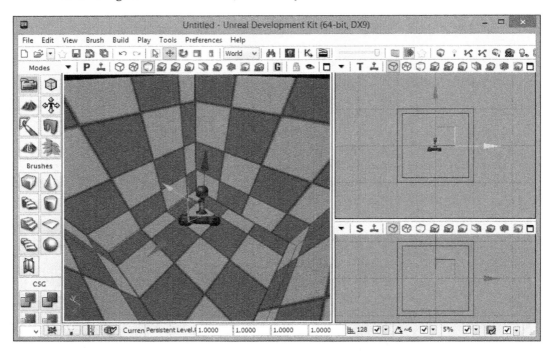

5. With **TowerDefenseMM** movie selected, open up Kismet. Create a level-loaded event by right-clicking and navigating to **New Event | Level Loaded**. To the right of that, create an Open GFx Movie action by right-clicking and navigating to **New Action | GFx UI | Open GFx Movie**.

6. Create a player variable for **Player Owner** by right-clicking and navigating to **New Variable | Player | Player**, and in the **Properties** tab uncheck the **All Players** option.

7. Create a new object variable for **Movie Player** by right-clicking on the pink arrow and navigating to **Create New Object Variable**. Left-click on the action to see its properties and with `TowerDefenseMM` Swf Movie selected in the content browser, click on the green arrow in the **Movie** property.

8. Connect **Loaded and Visible** from the **Level Loaded** event to **In** of the **Open GFx Movie** action.

   This will open the movie with the level and will show it on our player's screen.

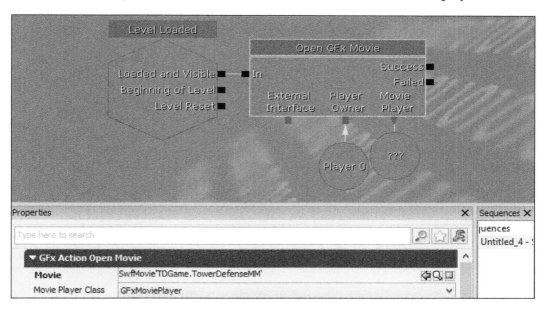

9. Next, create an `FSCommand` event by right-clicking and navigating to **New Event | GFx UI | FSCommand**. In the **Movie** option, select the same movie that we did previously. In the `FSCommand` property, type `playGame`, what we called in Flash as the argument for FSCommand.

10. To the right of the `FsCommand` event, create a **Console Command** action by right-clicking and navigating to **New Action | Misc | Console Command**. Inside the **[0]** property, fill the **open levelname** option, where level name is the name of your game level, which in my case is `Chapter04_TDGame`, and create a **Player** variable for the **Target**. Connect **Out** of **FsCommand** to **In** of the **Console Command** action.

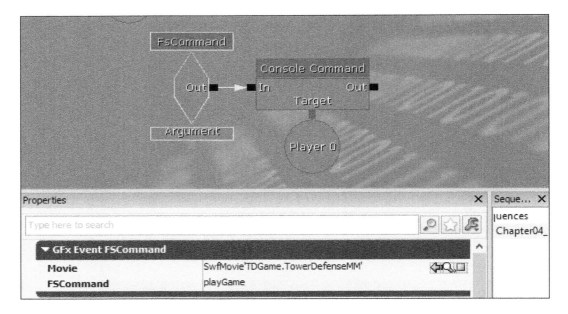

11. Build your project by navigating to **Build | Build All**. Save your game by navigating to **File | Save** and run our game by navigating to **Play | In Editor**.

Downloading the example code

You can download the example code files for all Packt books you have purchased from your account at `http://www.packtpub.com`. If you purchased this book elsewhere, you can visit `http://www.packtpub.com/support` and register to have the files e-mailed directly to you.

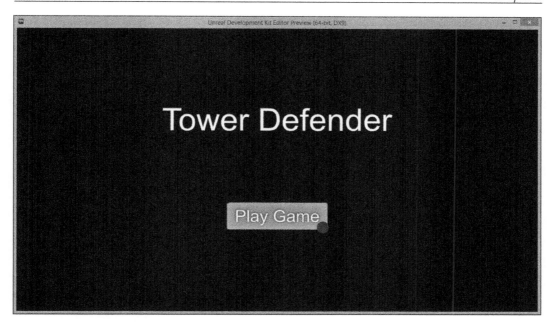

And with that our main menu is now fully functional! As of now, our button will not open a level due to the fact that the editor can't do it and that we haven't actually created the game's final map. However, if we opened the level inside of proper UDK, and the level name we stated exists, we'd head over to our next place.

Now that's great, but we still have one final thing to do, that is to bring the HUD into our actual game. Perform the following steps:

1. Now, open up the game that we finished at the end of the previous chapter.

2. With the `TowerDefenseHUDmovie` selected in the content browser, open up Kismet. Find the level-loaded event we created earlier with the **Console Command** beside it for the third-person perspective. To the right of that, create an Open GFx Movie action by right-clicking and navigating to **New Action | GFx UI | Open GFx Movie**.

3. Create a player variable for **Player Owner** by right-clicking and navigating to **New Variable | Player | Player**, and in **Properties** uncheck the **All Players** option.

4. Create a new object variable for Movie Player by right-clicking on the pink arrow and navigating to **Create New Object Variable**. Left-click on the action to see its properties and with **SwfMovie** selected in the content browser, click on the green arrow in the **Movie** property. Connect **Out** from the **Console Command** action to **In** of the **Open GFx Movie** action.

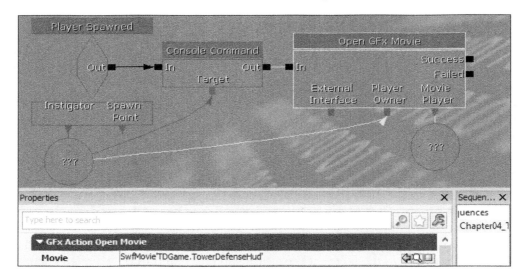

This is much like our previous section's Kismet, which will open the movie so that we can use it for different actions.

5. Next, each variable that we have created inside our Document Class will need to have its own variable inside of our Kismet. I created a comment (wrap) and pasted the variables inside its field. Then, for each variable, I created a global variable as you can see in the following screenshot:

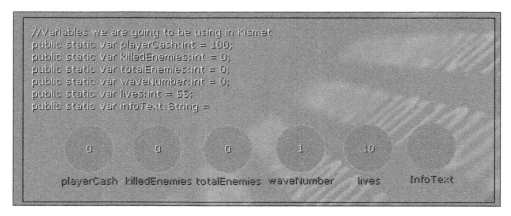

6. Add a `.1` second delay after the success of the **Open GFx Movie** action. So we give the movie a chance to load before we overwrite its data. The next step will be setting these variables. Besides the Open GFx Movie action, create a GFx SetVariable action (**New Action | GFx UI | GFx SetVariable**) and connect it from **Success** to **In** selecting the new **GFx SetVariable** action. Set the variable to `TowerDefenseHUD.playerCash`. Connect **Value** to our **playerCash** variable and connect the **Movie Player** variable to **Movie Player** from **Open GFx Movie**.

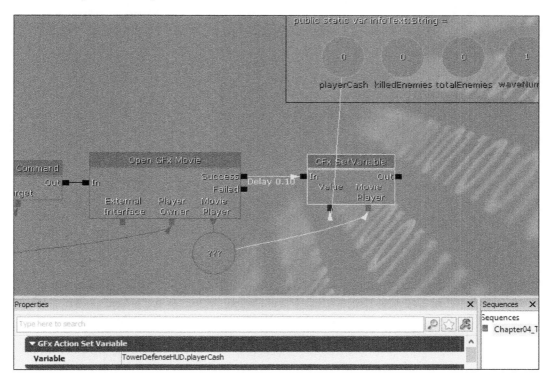

7. Once completed, do the same thing for all of the other variables that you have created. When you are finished, you should have something that looks like the following screenshot:

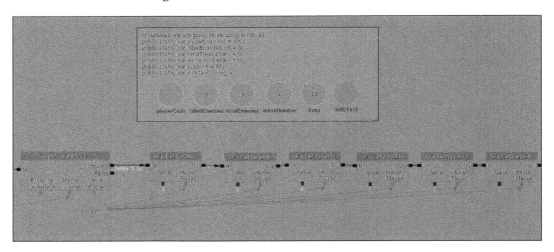

8. Now that we have initialized the variables, we will need to change them when they are needed to be changed. Go into Kismet and find the part in our Kismet where we incremented our wave number. From there, create a new **Named Variable** (**New Variable | Named Variable**) and give it the name `waveNumber`. Replace the connections from the previously created `waveNumber` and save.

9. Now create a GFx SetVariable action to connect to after we add one to the wave number. Connect **Movie Player** to the variable we created earlier in the Open GFx Movie action and **Value** to the **waveNumber** variable. Set the variable as `TowerDefenseHUD.waveNumber`.

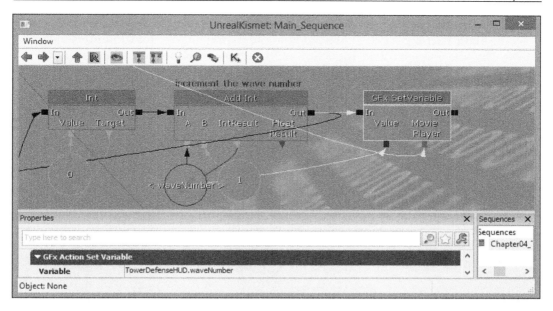

Variables will not be updated to our Flash side if we do not call GFx SetVariable because we set the text in the HUD based off of those values.

10. Next find all references to baseHealth and change its value to `lives`.

11. Similarly add **GFx SetVariable** to the end of it, updating its data on the HUD. After creating the **Subtract Int** event for **lives**, create a new GFx SetVariable event with the variable being `TowerDefenseHUD.lives` in order to update the HUD with the change.

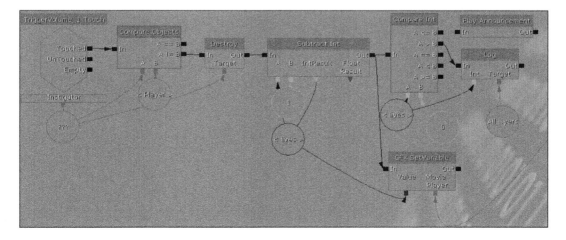

12. Whenever an enemy is created, we want the player to know about it. So after **Actor Factory** is called, we are going to increment our **totalEnemies** value by one using an **Add Int** action with itself as **IntResult** and then using **GFx SetVariable** in order to update the values in the `Scaleform` file.

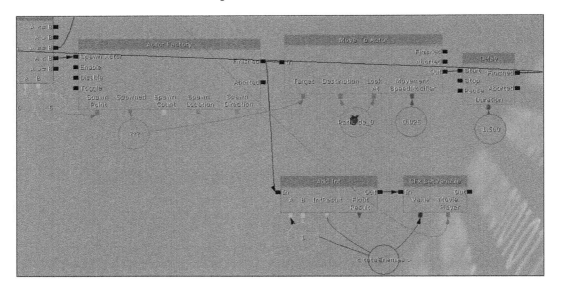

13. Next, whenever an enemy is killed or gets destroyed, we want to increment our **enemiesKilled** number. To do this, we will create a new event for Pawn Death (**New Event | Pawn | Death**).

14. Connect to the event the same **Add Int | GFx SetVariable** combo that we used previously for the variable `enemiesKilled` and `playerCash` with the variables being increased by 1 and 50 respectively.

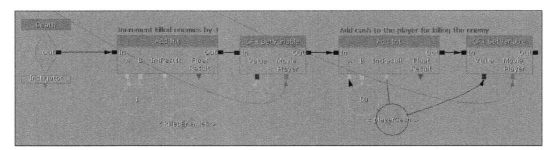

15. Now, after creating an enemy and incrementing the `totalEnemies` variable, create a new **Attach to Event** action (**New Action | Event | Attach to Event**) with the **Target** being the **Spawned** variable from **Actor Factory** and the **Event** to be the **Death** event that we just created. This means whenever an enemy that we spawn dies, we will gain money and increase the number of enemies that we killed.

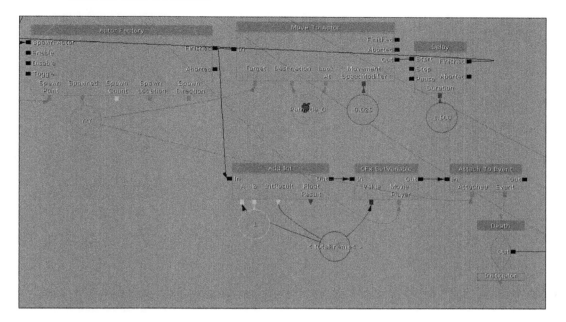

16. We also want the number to increase when they get destroyed. So, after we decrement our **lives** variable and set it, connect **Out** of the **GFx SetVariable** to the beginning of the **Death** event with the first **GFx SetVariable**.

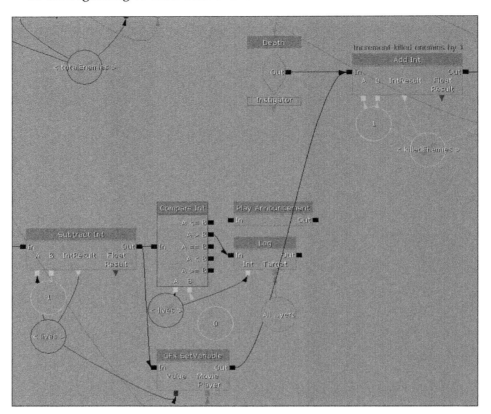

At the end of the code, we check to see if the player lost all of his lives where we had a **Play Announcement** action, but now let's delete that and replace it with something from our newly created HUD. I would like to replace it with a **GFx SetVariable** action changing our infoText to say **Game Over**.

17. After the GFx SetVariable action, create a delay of 0.5 seconds. Afterwards, create a **Console Command** to connect to it. Make a **Player** variable to connect to the **Target** variable and inside the properties of the **Console Command**, type quit in the first box for command. Now whenever the player loses all of his lives, he will see the **Game Over** text for a short period and the game will end.

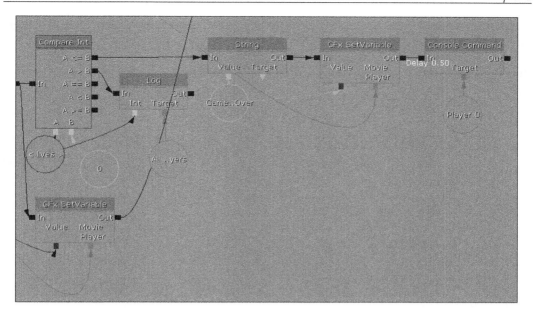

18. Build your project by navigating to **Build | Build All**. Save your game by navigating to **File | Save As** with the same level name as the open levelname command you created earlier. Now run your game by navigating to **Play | In Editor**.

And with that both our main menu and our HUD are now fully functional! Yes, there are plenty of other things we can do to extend or alter the gameplay, but it's a good idea to create a game that is uniquely your own. Note that, as of now, our button in the main menu will not open a level, due to the fact that the Editor can't do it; but we'll fix that shortly.

Cooking and packaging our game

At this point, you have all the beginnings of an amazing game. Once you are finished with your version of the game, you want to make it easy for people to download and play it; that's what packaging and cooking are for. Cooking makes the content consumer ready by compressing textures and doing a ton of different things to make the game ready to be installed on other systems, similar to a final compile. Cooking will also combine all your content packages into just a few files, a process that will also protect your content. It is impossible, or at least difficult, to extract things out of a cooked and combined package.

With that being said, let's get started! Perform the following steps:

1. Let's go back to the `ini` files and fix up some of them. Close the editor. You cannot change the `ini` files while the editor is running!

2. Open up `DefaultEngine.ini`. There you should see the text **Map=UDKFrontEnd.udk**.

    Change `UDKFrontEnd.udk` into our main menu level name instead. This will make it load your level by default. Thereafter, find the following code:

    `LocalMap=UDKFrontEnd.udk`

    And then perform the same steps, do the same thing as before.

3. You are done. Now select the `UDKEngine.ini` file and delete it. Doing this will force the engine to create a new `UDKEngine.ini` based on `DefaultEngine.ini`. Since you just modified the default ini, it will create a modified `UDKEngine.ini` with your changes in it. If you double-click on the `UDK.exe` file, you can verify that it loads your level.

4. To kick off the process, open up the `UnrealFrontEnd.exe` program, which is located in your `Binaries` folder of your UDK install.

5. Once you double-click on the icon, you can notice the field **Maps to cook**. Clear out this list and then add both of your levels here. At the **Launch Map** tab, check the **Override Default** option and select to use our main menu level as the starting point.

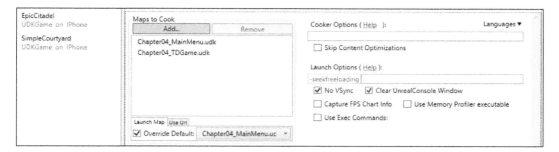

6. Next, we will want to enable **Package Game** so that we can create an installer for our game. To do this, go to the **Package Game** drop-down menu and select **Step Enabled**.

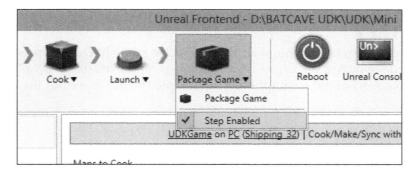

7. Finally, click on the **Start** button and wait for it to finish up. Once you get to the **Package Game** section, it will ask you some questions on what your game's name is and a shorter name it can go by.

8. The content in this folder is what will be distributed to the consumer. Now look in the main directory and you will find your consumer-ready-packaged game with the installer. Congrats! Your game is completed.

Taking the project to the next level

Our game is well on its way to being something special, but there are some things we could still add to make it even better! How about you take some time and try to complete the following:

- Add in a victory condition to the game, such as when we've reached wave 10, stop spawning enemies. If the player kills all of the enemies, he wins!

- Right now if you press *Esc* and exit the game you are brought to the default UDK menu. Overwrite this behavior through Kismet with a Key Pressed event.

- Have towers cost money in order to purchase them. This can easily be done by using Compare Int with your cash and as much you want to have towers cost.

- For those more interested in Scaleform or how to create more advanced projects, feel free to check out my previous book, *Mastering UDK Game Development*, also available from *Packt Publishing*, which has two additional chapters devoted to it.

Summary

And here we are! It's taken a bit of a time, but we've made it! Our game is now complete and we have a packaged version that we can distribute to people easily! Let's go through what we accomplished this chapter in which we did the following:

- Set up Flash for working with Scaleform
- Created a simple main menu screen
- Designed and implemented an HUD for gameplay
- Imported the files we created into UDK
- Finally got our game packaged using the Unreal Frontend

And from nothing to start with, let's take one last look at what we created:

I hope this book has inspired you to make games of your very own and gets you to a place where you are comfortable with making games within UDK. Game on!

Index

Symbols

F

Finished output 39
First Person Shooter (FPS) 31
Flash
  obtaining 92
  setting up 92
  URL 92
for loop 38
FSCommand 99
FSCommand event 109
FSCommand property 109

G

game
  cooking 120, 121
  packaging 120, 121
gameButton 93
Geometry mode 14
Geometry Mode button 13
Get Location and Rotation action 60
GFx SetVariable action 113, 118
GFx SetVariable event 115
Glow filter 95
Go to Builder Brush button 20
Grid snapping 12

H

Heads Up Display. *See* HUD
Hidden option 53
HUD
  about 91
  creating 100-106
hudInfoText 104
hudLives 103

I

Import button 107
information, classifying
  Kismet, advantages 29
  Kismet, disadvantages 30
  Kismet primer 28, 29
ini file 120
in-level boundaries
  adding 80-86

input 28

input 28
Instigator action 29
Instigator output 45, 46
Int action 42
Int Counter 37, 40

K

Kismet
  about 24, 25
  advantages 30
  disadvantages 30
Kismet primer
  about 28
  sequence object, parts 28

L

Level Loaded event 41, 109
lift off
  preparing 8
lives variable 118
Log action 50
Look At connector 39

M

marquee selection 13
materials
  applying 69-73
Max Trigger Count property 45, 55
menu
  creating 92-99
  creating, into UDK 107-120
MovementSpeedModifier variable 39
Move To Actor action 39, 40
Movie option 109
Movie Player variable 113

N

Named Variable 114
Name field 64, 93

O

object
  deleting 9
Object action 58

ObjectList object 36
OK button 93
Open GFx Movie action 112, 113
open levelname option 110
Out output 40, 42
output 28
Output Object connector 41
Oval tool 97
Over frame 94
Override Default option 121

P

Package field 64
Packages window 69
PathNode 34
Play Announcement action 49, 118
playButton 95
playerCash variable 113
Players Only option 45
Player Spawned event 44
Player variable 46, 118
playText 96
prefabs 63
project
  moving, to next level 122
Projectile Class property 61

R

restore viewports button 9

S

Scaleform
  installing, URL 92
Scaleform file 116
SCG (Switch Counter Groups) 64
Selection tool 97
sequence objects
  Actions object 29
  Conditions object 29
  Events object 29
  Variables object 29
Set Object Variable action 58
Spawned connector 39

Spawned output 36
Spawned variable 117
Spawn Projectile action 61
stair
  creating 74-79
  placing 73-79
Start button 121
Style section 103
Subtract Int action 47
Subtract Int event 115

T

Target variable 118
TDGame 107
Text tool 95, 102
thrusters
  engaging 9-27, 63-66
Toggle Hidden event 59
totalEnemies variable 117
Touch event 45
tower
  creating 52-63
  spawning 52-63
TowerDefenseHUDmovie 111
TowerDefensePKG package 64
Trigger_1 Used event 59
Trigger option 54
TriggerVolume_0 Touch event 46, 57, 58
Turret Target variable 57-60

U

UDK
  about 7, 69
  main menu, creating 107-120
  URL 8
UDKEngine.ini file 120
UDK.exe file 120
Unreal Development Kit. See UDK
UnrealFrontEnd.exe 120
UTPawn 36
UTPickupFactory 87
UT Sample Game option 8
utweapon 87

V

Variables object 29
Var Name property 42, 47
Volumes option 21

W

waveNumber variable 42, 114
WeaponFactories 87
weapons
  spawning 86-89

Thank you for buying
Getting Started with UDK

About Packt Publishing

Packt, pronounced 'packed', published its first book "*Mastering phpMyAdmin for Effective MySQL Management*" in April 2004 and subsequently continued to specialize in publishing highly focused books on specific technologies and solutions.

Our books and publications share the experiences of your fellow IT professionals in adapting and customizing today's systems, applications, and frameworks. Our solution based books give you the knowledge and power to customize the software and technologies you're using to get the job done. Packt books are more specific and less general than the IT books you have seen in the past. Our unique business model allows us to bring you more focused information, giving you more of what you need to know, and less of what you don't.

Packt is a modern, yet unique publishing company, which focuses on producing quality, cutting-edge books for communities of developers, administrators, and newbies alike. For more information, please visit our website: www.packtpub.com.

Writing for Packt

We welcome all inquiries from people who are interested in authoring. Book proposals should be sent to author@packtpub.com. If your book idea is still at an early stage and you would like to discuss it first before writing a formal book proposal, contact us; one of our commissioning editors will get in touch with you.

We're not just looking for published authors; if you have strong technical skills but no writing experience, our experienced editors can help you develop a writing career, or simply get some additional reward for your expertise.

UDK iOS Game Development Beginner's Guide

ISBN: 978-1-84969-190-1   Paperback: 280 pages

Create your own third-person shooter game using the Unreal Development Kit to create your own game on Apple's iOS devices, such as the iPhone, iPad, and iPod Touch

1. Learn the fundamentals of the Unreal Editor to create gameplay environments and interactive elements

2. Create a third-person shooter intended for the iOS and optimize any game with special considerations for the target platform

3. Take your completed game to Apple's App Store with a detailed walkthrough on how to do it

Grome Terrain Modeling with Ogre3D, UDK, and Unity3D

ISBN: 978-1-84969-939-6   Paperback: 162 pages

Create massive terrains and export them to the most pupular game engines

1. A comprehensive guide for terrain creation

2. Step-by-step walkthrough of Grome 3.1 and toolset

3. Export terrains to Unity3D, UDK, and Ogre3D

Please check **www.PacktPub.com** for information on our titles

Lightning Source UK Ltd.
Milton Keynes UK
UKOW05f0120150815

256945UK00010B/86/P

Getting Started with UDK

First published: July 2013

Production Reference: 1040713

Published by Packt Publishing Ltd.
Livery Place
35 Livery Street
Birmingham B3 2PB, UK.

ISBN 978-1-84969-981-5

www.packtpub.com

Cover Image by Abhishek Pandey (abhishek.pandey1210@gmail.com)

Getting Started with UDK

Blackburn
College

Library
01254 292120

Build a
using th

h

John P.

[PA

PUBL

BIRMINGHAM - MUMBAI